GERTRUDE STEIN

Women Writers

General Editors: *Eva Figes* and *Adele King*

Published titles

Margaret Atwood, Barbara Hill Rigney
Jane Austen, Meenakshi Mukherjee
Elizabeth Bowen, Phyllis Lassner
Anne Brontë, Elizabeth Langland
Charlotte Brontë, Pauline Nestor
Emily Brontë, Lyn Pykett
Fanny Burney, Judy Simons
Willa Cather, Susie Thomas
Colette, Diana Holmes
Ivy Compton-Burnett, Kathy Justice Gentile
Emily Dickinson, Joan Kirkby
George Eliot, Kristin Brady
Elizabeth Gaskell, Jane Spencer
Sylvia Plath, Susan Bassnet
Christina Stead, Diana Brydon
Gertrude Stein, Jane Palatini Bowers
Eudora Welty, Louise Westling
Edith Wharton, Katherine Joslin

Forthcoming

Elizabeth Barrett Browning, Marjorie Stone
Nadine Gordimer, Kathy Wagner
Doris Lessing, Margaret Moan Rowe
Katherine Mansfield, Diane DeBell
Toni Morrison, Nellie McKay
Jean Rhys, Carol Rumens
Christina Rossetti, Linda Marshall
Stevie Smith, Romana Huk
Virginia Woolf, Clare Hanson

Women Writers

Gertrude Stein

Jane Palatini Bowers

150th YEAR
M
MACMILLAN

First published 1993 by
THE MACMILLAN PRESS LTD
Houndmills, Basingstoke, Hampshire RG21 2XS
and London
Companies and representatives
throughout the world

ISBN 0–333–54909–0 hardcover
ISBN 0–333–54910–4 paperback

A catalogue record for this book is available
from the British Library

Printed in Hong Kong

Contents

Acknowledgements

I would like to thank Betsy Gitter, Carol Stanger, Peggy Escher and Marcia Silver for their insightful reading of my work and for their invaluable suggestions for its improvement. The writing of this book was supported in part by grants from The Research Foundation of the City University of New York and from the Northeast Modern Language Association, and I am grateful for their assistance. Finally, I thank my daughter Chloë who lived with me while I wrote and who made sure that, in the words of Gertrude Stein, 'living was all loving'.

The author and publishers wish to thank the following who have kindly given permission for the use of copyright material: Random House, Inc. for extracts from *Selected Writings of Gertrude Stein* by Gertrude Stein, copyright 1946 by Random House, Inc.; the Estate of Gertrude Stein for extracts from *The Making of Americans* by Gertrude Stein; Yale University Press for 'Can You See the Name' from *Bee Time Vine and Other Pieces*, 1953, pp. 204–5 by Gertrude Stein; and the Yale Collection of American Literature, Beinecke Rare Book and Manuscript Library, Yale University, for extracts from the Gertrude Stein papers in its collections.

Every effort has been made to trace all the copyright holders but if any have been inadvertently overlooked the publishers will be pleased to make the necessary arrangement at the first opportunity.

Editors' Preface

The study of women's writing has been long neglected by a male critical establishment both in academic circles and beyond. As a result, many women writers have either been unfairly neglected or have been marginalised in some way, so that their true influence and importance has been ignored. Other women writers have been accepted by male critics and academics, but on terms which seem, to many women readers of this generation, to be false or simplistic. In the past the internal conflicts involved in being a woman in a male-dominated society have been largely ignored by readers of both sexes, and this has affected our reading of women's work. The time has come for a serious reassessment of women's writing in the light of what we understand today.

This series is designed to help in that reassessment.

All the books are written by women because we believe that men's understanding of feminist critique is only, at best, partial. And besides, men have held the floor for quite long enough.

EVA FIGES
ADELE KING

For my mother and for Lila

Introduction

Describing her own work in *Everybody's Autobiography*, Gertrude Stein comments: 'My writing is clear as mud, but mud settles and clear streams run on and disappear' (104). As we consider Stein's work in the pages that follow, reader be warned: We will be digging in the mud. That is, we will focus on Stein's experimental writing, the work that presents the greatest difficulty for readers.

Stein did produce a few clear flowing streams in her life, most of them in her last decade. Works like *The Autobiography of Alice B. Toklas* and *Lectures in America*, for example, were motivated by an autobiographical urge, a need to explain herself to a public that had consistently rejected her work, to assert her own centrality in the modernist movement in arts and letters, and to justify a lifetime spent pursuing a programme of literary experimentation that was at once the basis of her marginality and of her claims for centrality. Because their purpose was to explain her life and her poetics, these works are among the most readable Stein ever wrote. However, they are not the source of her enduring value as a writer; thus, they will not concern us here. We will consider instead several of her early narratives, her first book of poems and some representative plays from two decades of playwriting. These are works that have, as Stein puts it, 'settled'; they are also works that often seem 'clear as mud' to readers.

I divide Stein's corpus generically because Stein had an abiding interest in genre, as she did in other systems which limit a writer's creativity and by which readers classify a writer's work. As she pushed against the constraints imposed by the conventions of genre, so she questioned the rules that confine language within preordained structures and that dictate the use of literature as a means of representation. Her interest in literary systems was to subvert and dismantle them, creating in the process works that stretch the limits of literary form and challenge the reader in a uniquely conscious and provocative way.

In the energy, irreverence and extremity of her experimentation, Stein is closer to the painters than to the writers of the modernist period. Though she was a voracious reader, she seems to have been indifferent to the work of her contemporaries and fellow literary experimenters – Joyce, Woolf and Pound, for example – and her own work shows little of their influence. Nonetheless, she shares with these other modernists an interest in deconstructing the forms of language and literature and a self-reflexive concern with the process of writing.

Although Stein always begins a work as a representational task set within generic boundaries – to record the history of a family's progress in a novel; to depict objects, food and rooms (domestic details) in a series of 'verbal still lifes'; to convey 'the essence of what happened' in a play – her re-creation of external reality always erupts into linguistic recreation. Stein's attention to representation is diverted by her enjoyment of language play; she writes within a genre only to re-generate and transform it. Her writing thus celebrates the recreational and generative aspects of language. Stein also celebrates her own performance as a writer. Normally, literature is the result of a sequence of events, the composing process, that is not available to us as we read the text. By contrast, Stein's texts inscribe her performance as a writer and that performance replaces all other events as the focus of the text. The construction of the work is revealed to us; we are invited to witness the writer writing. Whether the work is a narrative, a lyric or a drama, it is ultimately a performance by Gertrude Stein, the writer. Stein invents a kind of 'process poetics' that informs all of her work.

Once writing is written, however, process necessarily becomes product. Stein's work reveals and revels in this doubleness of writing – that it is at once performance act and material fact. At the same time that she plays with the instability of language, she confronts its fixity. Looking at the composition as an object, she arranges and rearranges its parts and describes it contours (how words are spelled, for example, or how many lines she has written). While she is representing the subject, playing with language, deconstructing and re-generating the genre and contemplating the composition, she is also announcing, demonstrating and evaluating her own poetics. She is at once the writer and the reader of her own text, at once a practitioner and a critic.

Stein's texts demonstrate and comment upon the complexity of the creative act. The multi-layered compositions to which this book will introduce you have influenced other writers not because they invite formal imitation (no one writes quite like Gertrude Stein) but because they address the problems and paradoxes at the heart of language and of literary creation.

1 The Half That Made Her: 1874–1909

And so I am an American and I have lived half my
life in Paris, not the half that made me but the half
in which I made what I made.

'An American and France' (WAM 62)

I

In 1909 Gertrude Stein's first published work, *Three Lives*,
appeared in print. She was thirty-five years old, living with
her brother Leo, two years her senior, in their two-story
Parisian apartment at 27, rue de Fleurus. In the atelier
adjacent to the apartment hung their ever-growing collection of modern art which by 1909 included works by
Toulouse-Lautrec, Gaugin, Renoir, Degas and Cézanne.
The Steins were among the first to collect Cézanne, and
they had two compositions of bathers, a still life with apples,
a water color of Montagne Sainte-Victoire and a portrait of
Madame Cézanne seated in a red chair and holding a fan,
a portrait which Stein later said had inspired her as she sat
beneath it writing *Three Lives*. The Steins were almost alone
at the time in collecting Matisse and Picasso, and the walls
of the atelier displayed, among others, Matisse's *Woman
with the Hat*, *Joy of Life* and *The Blue Nude*, and Picasso's
Young Girl with Basket of Flowers, *Seated Woman with Hood*,
Dozing Absinthe Drinker (from his Blue period), *Boy Leading
a Horse* and *Young Acrobat on a Ball* (from his Rose period),
several of the large rose nudes and, of course, *Portrait of*

Gertrude Stein. According to Stein, it was while walking home from her eighty or ninety sittings for this portrait that she had composed the stories collected in *Three Lives.*

Every Saturday evening brother and sister were 'at home' in the atelier, making their collection and themselves available to the gaze of the curious, some of whom were fascinated and some repelled by what they saw. The only condition of admission was that you be brought or sent by a friend of the Steins. So it was that Alfred Stieglitz, the American photographer, came to visit at 27, rue de Fleurus, attracted by stories of the fabulous art collection and brought by Edward Steichen, also an American photographer, then living in Paris. Stieglitz described this visit in a later conversation:

I found myself in a huge room. Paintings covered the walls from floor nearly to ceiling. . . .

Books and papers covered a long table, very long, at which sat a bald man with eyeglasses and whiskers. Elsewhere in the room I noticed a woman, dark and bulksome.

Steichen introduced me to the man, Leo Stein, and to the woman, whose name I did not hear. No one else was present.

I stood . . . some distance to the left of Stein; Steichen, in the other corner, to the right, partly hidden from him. The woman half reclined on a chaise longue.

Leo Stein began to talk. I quickly realized I had never heard more beautiful English nor anything clearer. He held forth on art. He must have spoken for at least an hour and a half.[1]

Although he had been impressed by Leo Stein's speaking, Stieglitz later told Steichen that what had been 'most remarkable about the visit to [Leo] Stein was the woman. She appeared to understand everything the man said and oftentimes smiled a knowing smile. But she never spoke a word'.[2] It wasn't until years later, when he was about to publish two of her verbal portraits in his magazine, *Camera Work*, that Stieglitz realized that the dark woman in the chaise longue had been Gertrude Stein. In recounting this story to her when he met her again in 1934 during her lecture tour of the United States, he said that he had never known anyone to sit still for so long without saying a word.[3]

Stieglitz's impression of Gertrude Stein in this period is corroborated by other visitors to the atelier. Even Alice Toklas, who was soon to know Gertrude intimately, noted that during their first meeting she laughed 'a good deal', but talked 'very little'.[4] As one friend reflected, 'Most of the visitors to the Stein apartment in 1909 paid little attention to Gertrude. The center of attraction was Leo's brilliant conversation on modern French art'.[5] Few people knew that Stein was writing regularly and seriously and that she had recently published the three stories that would be acknowledged later as the earliest modernist, experimental fiction (predating James Joyce's *Dubliners* by five years and Virginia Woolf's *Jacob's Room* by thirteen). Who could have guessed that beneath the silent and serene exterior lay a reservoir of words about to gush forth in an unstoppable fountain, a torrent of writing which could all but drown the talkative brother. Leo did not then know that he was about to lose this sister, who, as a close friend put it, 'admired and loved him in a way a man is seldom admired and loved'.[6] In 1909 this listener in the house, Leo's captive ear for thirty-five years, was about to turn away from him for good.

II

The closeness between brother and sister had been fostered by the circumstances of their birth and cemented during their childhood by the near-absence of adult and peer influence. Leo and Gertrude were the last of seven children born to Daniel and Amelia Keyser Stein; two of the seven had died in infancy, and in fact, Leo and Gertrude had been conceived, so it was told in the family, to take the place of the two dead children, a morbid exchange of death for life that was to become the theme of many Steinian literary meditations. The two children nearest in age to Leo and Gertrude (Bertha, four years, and Simon, seven years older than Gertrude) were temperamentally and intellectually no match for their exceedingly volatile and verbal younger siblings. The eldest brother, Michael, was not much involved in the life of the youngest children until he assumed their guardianship in their late teens when Daniel Stein died. Although both the Steins and Keysers were large extended families living primarily in Baltimore (with branches in New York and Pittsburgh), Daniel and Amelia Stein had quarrelled with Daniel's brother and business partner, Solomon, and with Solomon's wife, Pauline. Because of this quarrel, the Daniel Stein family lived in Europe (in Vienna and in Passy, France) for the first five years of Gertrude's life and then removed permanently to Oakland, California in 1880 when she was six. They lived in a neighbourhood of poor working-class people (the only Jews, the only rich family), and the children did not regularly attend school because Daniel Stein frequently engaged private tutors for them or neglected their schooling altogether.

Amelia Stein died of cancer when Gertrude was fourteen, but she had been ill with the disease for many years before her death and seems to have been a shadowy and insubstantial presence in the lives of her youngest children. Daniel Stein had a more forceful impact on his children, but he was erratic in his attention and unpredictable in his responses and therefore not a steady influence. Although Leo complained bitterly later in his life about their father's autocratic rule and violent temper, Gertrude seems to have been able to avoid confronting him, if not actually, at least imaginatively. Her handling of her father is the first example of a propensity she demonstrated throughout her life to 'write' people off (literally and figuratively). Once estranged from people, she acted as though they had never meant very much to her, writing about them and behaving toward them as though she hardly remembered them, almost as if they had never existed. Thus, whereas Leo writes in his notes toward an autobiography – 'My memories . . . . from my third to my sixth year, are numerous, and with few exceptions they are unpleasant. . . . My recollections of my father at this time are also almost all disagreeable'[7] – Stein writes in *Everybody's Autobiography*, 'About an unhappy childhood well I never had an unhappy anything. . . . My brother and I had had everything. Gradually he was remembering that his childhood had not been a happy one. My eldest brother and I had not had that impression, certainly not' (59). Yet elsewhere in this autobiography, she substantiates Leo's perception of Daniel Stein. 'Naturally,' she writes, 'My father was not satisfied with anything . . . . Naturally our father was very often irritated' (118). However, she reports this paternal dissatisfaction and irritation as directed against her brothers – especially the eldest, Michael – not against herself. Though she implies that Daniel Stein had not in fact made her childhood unhappy, she also concludes that fathers are 'depressing'. She blames the ills of the world on an excess of fathers, men like Hitler and Stalin, for example, 'looming and filling up everything' (113). Regarding her own father's death in 1891, she writes with artful understatement: 'Then our life without a father began a very pleasant one' (121) – a more devastating assessment of life with a father than any that Leo rendered in his reminiscences of that life.

Given the isolated circumstances of their lives, brother and sister relied solely on each other for companionship and entertainment, and in the case of the younger sister, for 'guidance'. Stein describes the relationship in *Everybody's Autobiography*: 'My brother led in everything. . . . He had always been my brother two years older and a brother. I had always been following' (59). Gertrude Stein's biographer, James Mellow, makes much of her dependence on Leo, but more recently, in *Women of the Left Bank*, Shari Benstock has suggested that 'Leo Stein may have needed to be central to Gertrude's life, rather than she to his.'[8] Based on the evidence, it is more reasonable to suppose that the two had a mutual dependence that served each very well for a time but that eventually became so debilitating for Gertrude that she had to eliminate Leo from her life and her consciousness (much as she had done with their father and the unhappy parts of her childhood).

In her early writing Stein explored in apparent fascination the twin themes of independence and dependence. She had mapped a characterology of everyone she knew based on the mixture of independence and dependence in each personality. As for Stein, she identified herself in *Everybody's Autobiography* as a 'person of no initiative, I usually stay where I am', she writes (94).[9] In an early, thinly-disguised autobiographical novel (*Q.E.D.*), she represented herself as the slow, unadventurous, acquiescent character, Adele, the one who was more dependent than independent and ponderous to the point of immobility. In *The Autobiography of Alice B. Toklas*, Stein writes, 'She [Gertrude Stein] has a great deal of inertia and once started keeps going until she starts somewhere else' (82).[10]

Leo seems to have been her opposite in this regard. He changed careers and residences with unusual frequency. A theme of his early letters is his inability to fix on any one interest long enough to develop it. If she had no initiative, then he had more than enough for two. If she normally stayed where she was, then he was able to pull her after him in his peripatetic search for a place that would not bore him. His nervous irritability and physical restlessness may have acted on her as a kind of tonic, offering her an escape from her own sometimes depressed torpor. For him she seems to have provided a steadying influence. He thought of her as absorbing and holding in a kind of mental entropy the ideas and interests that so easily side-tracked him. In a condescending but revealing letter to her in December 1900, he explained why he preferred Florence, 'where a limited range of activity is almost insisted on', to New York, 'where everything is on the go', and he connected his preference for Florence to his own easily distracted and indecisive mind. He compared himself to her:

> I can get nowhere decisively. You see I'm unteachable, therefore I have to examine everything for myself and I can't, as you do, rest with a good many things in my mind really unexamined and a good many others solved by an easy conventional solution.[11]

Here and elsewhere Leo suggests (not very subtly) that his own 'wild scramble to find answers' is superior to his sister's supposedly conventional and unreflecting acceptance of things as they are. However much it demeaned her, he seemed to rely on this conception of her calm, if limited mental activity as a necessary counterbalance to his own wild indecisiveness, and Stein seems to have accepted his characterization of her. As he resided in the limited city of Florence, so he 'resided' with a limited version of his sister in order to remove himself from 'too various a field', to save 'time and energy' and to achieve 'results'.[12]

Stein did in fact provide a place for Leo to reside: first, as a medical student in Baltimore where, as she told Sarah Stein, the wife of their brother Michael, she was 'going to keep house and nurse him [Leo] according to all the latest medical school theories';[13] and later, after she had left medical school, in Paris at rue de Fleurus, where they were, as one friend referred to them somewhat sardonically, 'the happiest couple on the Left Bank'.[14] To Leo, Gertrude may also have symbolized home; she may herself have been the imaginary locus of a kind of mythic home, a place where he could 'live happily ever after' as he described his and Gertrude's eventual and imagined American retirement to 'Connecticut or Duxbury or somewhere'.[15] Whenever and wherever he thought of settling, he always planned to install Gertrude in that place, and she would always appear as called for (though she was not always willing to remain). For both Steins, then, the myth of the dependent/dependable sister and the independent/undependable brother served a psychic purpose. However, there were emotional, sexual and intellectual forces at work in Gertrude Stein that made the myth difficult to sustain.

In a poignant prelapsarian evocation of their childhood together, Stein reveals simultaneously the pleasures and the problems of the 'family romance' as she experienced it. She writes:

My brother and myself had always been together. . . . My brother and I were always together. . . . It is better if you are the youngest girl in a family to have a brother two years older, because that makes everything a pleasure to you, you go everywhere and do everything while he does it all for and with you which is a pleasant way to have everything happen to you. . . . He learned to read first and I learned to read after. . . . He found a good many books that I would not have found and I read a great many books that did not interest him but I did read a great many of the books that he found. . . . When we were very little children we went many miles on dusty roads in California together, all alone together and he would shoot a jack rabbit and then I would try to shoot after he had shot it. . . . It was all as it could have been. (EA 54–7)

Following her brother meant that she could not herself lead.
If she accepted his leadership, she was able to find things
that she might not otherwise have found (here books), but
there was no reciprocation. She found books, too, but these
did not interest him as the ones that he found interested
her. This pattern was to be repeated throughout their life
together. The more interested Stein became in what she was
herself discovering in those areas into which Leo had led
her, the more independent she became of Leo's influence;
though her independence seems to have frightened her
because it ruined everything 'as it could have been', she
found ways to allay her fears, usually through the agency
of a third person. As she became less frightened of the self
she was defining and as she found validation of this self in
others, he appeared to feel increasingly threatened by her
independent discoveries. His supposed indifference to her
and to her discoveries became an ingrained self-defensive
posture. By dismissing her endeavours as uninteresting, he
could effectively undercut her moves toward independence,
at least for a time.

The first stage on which the two played out this family
drama was Harvard University, where Leo had enrolled
in 1892 and Gertrude in 1893, at Radcliffe, the Harvard
Annex for women, then called The Society for the Colle-
giate Instruction of Women; both Leo and Gertrude were
philosophy majors. Although Stein's biographer describes
her at this time as trailing after Leo 'like a satellite after a
superior planet'[16] and although pictures of the two from
this period show her always with her hand securely tucked
into the crook of his arm, in her four years at Harvard she
made her first attempt to define her own orbit beyond the
sphere of Leo's influence.

In her freshman year Stein enrolled in Philosophy I
in which William James lectured on psychology, then
considered a branch of philosophy. Leo had already 'discovered' James and, true to form, Gertrude had followed

her brother's interest. But by his own account, Leo was already tiring of philosophy and had at that time no interest in psychology, and although he continued to read and admire James throughout his life, in 1893 he was distracted from philosophy by his new interest in history. Gertrude, on the other hand, took seven courses from James, enrolling five times in his Philosophy 20a, a course in experimental psychology normally open only to graduate students. From all reports, James was an engaging teacher and a stimulating and supportive mentor. He found Stein to be an admirable student, and he soon had her working collaboratively and independently on experiments on attention span and automatic response. To borrow her biographer's metaphor, James was a new planet around which Gertrude could orbit, a potential substitute for the brother she had been in the habit of following. While she was James's student, she seems to have been devoted to him, writing in a college English theme, 'Is life worth living? Yes, a thousand times yes when the world still holds such spirits as Prof. James. He is truly a man among men'.[17] Numerous critics have pointed to the influence of James's ideas on her work, especially her early work,[18] and Stein herself spoke throughout her life of her admiration for James, whom she called a 'great teacher', and of the influence he had on her in college and in her later life.

From a practical point of view, James's inclusion of Stein in his psychology laboratory enlarged her circle of friends beyond the group to which Leo had introduced her. She consolidated these friendships when Leo left Cambridge in late fall 1895 for a trip around the world with their cousin, Fred Stein. In his absence Stein became secretary of the Philosophy Club, attended the symphony regularly with a group of her friends and conducted experiments with a friend and graduate student, Leon Solomons, the results of which the two wrote up and published as 'Normal Motor Automatism' in the September 1896 issue of the

Harvard Psychological Review. Most importantly, following
James's advice and without apparently consulting Leo,
Stein decided to attend medical school at Johns Hopkins
since she wished to become, like her mentor, a psychologist,
and since, as she later reported in *The Autobiography of Alice
B. Toklas*, this was the course of study he had recommended
to her.

Meanwhile, Leo had written from Cairo in March 1896
to coax her into joining him that summer for a tour of
the Lowlands, Germany and Paris. Though he urged
her to make her plans quickly (especially to apply to
their brother Michael for a letter of credit), she seems
to have 'stalled', for in June Michael was writing to her
to chastise her gently for not having made her travel
arrangements. Nevertheless, she did eventually join Leo
in Italy, a country he had in the meantime 'discovered'.
Brother and sister returned to Cambridge in the fall,
Gertrude to finish up her last year of college and Leo
to cast about for a new direction. His choice reveals the
interdependence of the two siblings. Having previously
shown little or no interest in biology, Leo now decided
to pursue some independent biological research at Johns
Hopkins, spurred on, no doubt, by Gertrude's impending
entrance into medical school there.

So the two arrived in Baltimore in 1897 and set up
housekeeping together. For the next two years Stein studied
and did well in her medical school courses. Leo characteris-
tically lost interest in biology and 'one day . . . got a great
idea in aesthetics', an idea he decided to pursue further in
Florence.[19] In 1900, then, after a summer of travelling in
Europe with his sister and a mutual friend, he settled in
Florence, where he was to remain, on and off, for two
years.

Between the moment of his great idea and the event of
his expatriation, he continued to live with his sister, whose
grades began to slip in the year before his departure. In

the year following his departure, she failed four of her nine courses, and though she returned to Johns Hopkins in 1901 to do brain tract research, her medical career was effectively over. It is not entirely clear why Stein failed her courses and then abandoned medical school. It would have been possible for her to make up the courses she had failed, but this she refused to do. Richard Bridgman accepts Stein's own explanation: that the first two years interested her because they involved laboratory work but that the practice and theory of medicine, undertaken in the last two years, bored her. James Mellow suggests that 'Leo's defection contributed to the failure of . . . [her] medical career', but Shari Benstock has rightly pointed out that her grades had shown 'a marked decline' before Leo's expatriation.[20] Stein may very well have realized that medicine was not her calling, but her loss of interest may also be explained by the dynamic of her relationship with Leo.

In 1934, years after their Baltimore experience, in one of many letters he wrote denouncing Stein's *Autobiography of Alice B. Toklas* as 'oodles of bosh', Leo discusses her attitude toward her medical studies:

Gertrude used to have a sense of humor with regard to herself. Of her 'research' work at medical school she made fun at the time, saying that the women who were at Johns Hopkins for the first time fell in with Mall's hobby for making models of the brain tracts, to show how interested they were; that the men wouldn't waste their time on it. She told me that she didn't mind doing it, as it was purely mechanical work and rather restful. She told me then how a German anatomist to whom Mall showed these models said it was an excellent occupation for women and Chinamen, and Gertrude quite agreed. ['Mall' refers to Franklin P. Mall, Professor of Anatomy][21]

Assuming that Leo's recollection is correct and that Stein did make fun of her own endeavours, her self-deprecating humour may have been a way for her to participate in Leo's dismissal of her efforts as 'uninteresting' and to make those efforts less threatening to him and to her. After all, the same woman who supposedly agreed that 'her work was an excellent occupation for women and Chinamen' had had the results of her student dissection of an infant brain included (with attribution) in Dr. Llewellys Barker's *The Nervous System and Its Constituent Neurons* (1899). This same woman had returned to Johns Hopkins after failing her courses, specifically to continue her work under the auspices of Dr. Barker, who assured her in a letter that 'it would seem a pity not to [continue], now that you have gone so far in this line of work and have so good a back-ground'.[22]

In February 1901, having heard of her desire to abandon her studies, Leo wrote: 'It would be too bad if the first person in the family who had gone so far as to get adequate preparation for anything should go back on it'.[23] Coming from the one person in the family obsessed with his inability to complete anything (his 'terrific neurosis' as he came to call it), this letter which some see as 'encouraging'[24] must, on the contrary, have been quite unsettling. Stein was not yet ready to assert her own authority at her brother's expense. In 1902 she gave up her research work and in 1903 followed Leo to Paris and to rue de Fleurus where he had moved to begin his new career as a painter. After a brief visit to America in 1904, Stein commenced an expatriation that was to last thirty years.

III

Between 1900, when Leo left Baltimore, and 1904, when Stein settled in permanently at rue de Fleurus, her life was transformed, as it had been at Harvard, by events that transpired in her brother's absence. This time the transformation was to prove definitive, and its effects were to last a lifetime.

As had happened at Harvard, Leo had no sooner departed than Gertrude began to expand her circle of friends. She began to meet regularly with a group of women, mostly graduates of eastern women's colleges, at the Baltimore apartment of Mabel Haynes and Grace Lounsbery, where the women would have tea and lively discussions about moral and intellectual issues.[25] Though all the women in this circle, except Stein, were eventually to marry, evidence suggests that some of them were experiencing homosexual stirrings and were questioning, if only privately, their own possible deviation from conventional sexual mores. It was in this setting that Stein met May Bookstaver, with whom she fell in love. Her on-again, off-again affair with Bookstaver was to last for three years, though it took Stein an additional year and a half after their final separation to get over the effects of their involvement.[26] The affair was complicated in part by the fact that Bookstaver was more experienced than Stein in such matters and was alternately amused and annoyed at Stein's naïveté and earnestness. Because she was more experienced, she was less apprehensive and more self-assured than Stein, who seems to have been almost paralysed by her initial repugnance toward her own developing sexuality. The affair was further complicated by the presence of a rival, the very Mabel Haynes who hosted the weekly tea parties at which Stein had met Bookstaver. According to Stein's fictional account of the affair in *Q.E.D.* and as suggested in letters to Stein from other friends in the circle, Bookstaver encouraged the attentions of both women while committing herself to neither. The tumultuous course of this romance may have been yet another factor in Stein's inability or unwillingness to complete medical school.

As difficult as it was, however, the affair had the positive effect of awakening Stein's previously slumbering sexuality and leading her to discover a passionate self she had long repressed. This sexual self-discovery and self-definition were not without conflict, a conflict intensified, no doubt, by the fact that the new feelings were homo-erotic. In *Q.E.D.*, Adele (the Stein character) is torn between her desire to yield herself 'to the complete joy' of being with Helen (the Bookstaver character) and her 'fierce disgust' at this yielding. In one scene in which the two have 'lost themselves in happiness' Adele is 'aroused . . . by a kiss that seemed to scale the very walls of chastity'. Instead of abandoning herself to the sensation, 'she flung away on the instant filled with battle and revulsion' (FQED 102). Adele later analyses the moment and her revulsion:

My instincts . . . have always been opposed to the indulgence of any feeling of passion. I suppose that is due to the Calvinistic influence that dominates American training and has interfered with my natural temperament. Somehow you have made me realise that my attitude in the matter was degrading and material, instead of moral and spiritual but in spite of you my puritan instincts again and again say no and I get into a horrible mess. I am beginning to distrust my instincts and I am about convinced that my objection was not a deeply moral one. I suppose after all it was a good deal cowardice. (FQED 103)[27]

Adele realizes that the self-loathing occasioned by her homo-erotic desires does not derive from any 'moral theory' of right and wrong or from a concern with the world's opinion, which Adele declares she does not 'regard', but from 'cowardice'. This realization would free her, if she would be but brave enough, to act on her sexual attraction for Helen. By characterizing Adele's – and her own – disgust as a function of fearfulness, Stein seems to have been able to free herself from the moral and societal pressures that had prevented her from accepting and enjoying her sexuality before and during her affair with Bookstaver. That affair, turbulent and doomed though it was, brought Stein to accept her own sexual orientation and to define herself as a lesbian.

At the same time that she was dealing with the consequences of her feelings for Bookstaver, Stein was beginning to write fiction and to think of herself as a writer. This new vocation seems to have been prompted in part by her need to understand the contradictory impulses that had motivated her conflicted behaviour toward Bookstaver.

In 1902, in the throes of the relationship with May Bookstaver, Stein joined Leo, as she usually did, for a summer of European travel. She planned to spend the entire year abroad, in part to put some distance between herself and Bookstaver. After a summer in Florence, Leo and Gertrude went to England where, according to Mellow, they intended to stay for five or six months.[28] During the cold and damp English winter, Stein spent her days in the reading room of the British Museum. She immersed herself in a program of reading which Leon Katz describes as a kind of education in British narrative 'from the sixteenth century to the present'.[29] She kept lists of her reading and copied passages into a set of notebooks she had bought for the purpose. In addition she began keeping in these notebooks a record of 'memories, observations, quotations, and story material'.[30] These activities suggest that she was preparing herself for her own venture into narrative. Earlier, in a conversation with a friend of Leo's who had asked her why she never thought of becoming a critic since she 'spoke so intelligently about writing', she had replied: 'As a matter of fact, I did, long ago, but I found that analysis is not in my line. I'll leave that to Leo – he loves to chew the cud. I want to do something more vital than write about the writing of others'.[31] Having safely left literary analysis

to Leo and having studied 'the writing of others', Stein
was ready in 1903 to begin the 'vital' work of creating the
writing that others would study.

In New York in February 1903, after fleeing the London
winter and the depression that had settled on her while she
had lived there with Leo, Stein began to write *The Making of
Americans*, a novel about a 'typical' middle-class American
family with recent immigrant roots and solid bourgeois
values, a fictional family based loosely on a branch of
her own family. In writing about this family, Stein was
able to explore that side of her nature that she thought of
as American and Anglo-Saxon, the side that she believed
had made her resistant to her attraction for Bookstaver.
In the same year (1903) that she began this novel, she
wrote *Q.E.D.*, in which she recounts the troubled affair
with Bookstaver and tries to account for its unhappy end.
It is not clear from the evidence whether Stein began
Q.E.D. in New York, in Florence where she again spent
the summer with Leo, or at rue de Fleurus where she moved
in September 1903, but wherever and whenever she began
it, she finished it in Paris shortly after her arrival. Both
Mellow and Bridgman have called the writing of *Q.E.D.*
therapeutic.[32] Clearly, *Q.E.D.* and the early chapters of *The
Making of Americans* were autobiographical fictions through
the writing of which Stein was trying to understand herself
and her life.

The sister Leo had left in Baltimore was not the same
sister who moved in with him in Paris in 1903, but it is
not likely that he knew of either her sexual or her vocational
transformation. It seems that, at this time, he was unaware
of her lesbianism (or at least not consciously aware).
Though the two talked incessantly, their conversation
seems to have centered primarily on ideas with some
gossiping about mutual friends. From his letters to her we
can see that he was fairly forthright about his own affairs,
but since he was developing a habit of talking and she of

listening, it is possible he never heard of hers. At least, so it appears from the record.[33] About her writing, Stein seems to have been equally reticent. It wasn't until some time later that she showed him *The Making of Americans*, and, as for *Q.E.D.*, she put that manuscript away in a cupboard of the rue de Fleurus apartment where it remained for the next thirty years. Whatever writing she did while she lived with Leo at rue de Fleurus, she did at night after he had retired. She wrote until the sun came up and then went to bed. Whatever confidences she made of her feelings for Bookstaver were made to her women friends in person and in letters. Thus, she had created a life separate from Leo, and though she lived with him, she also lived alone with her 'secret' affair and her 'secret' writing. One wonders whether her increasing silence in her brother's presence, the silence so remarkable to Stieglitz and others who met the two in 1909, was not the result of this burden of secrecy, for she who carries secrets may become mute for fear of giving something away.

IV

In 1905 in the gallery of Clovis Sagot, an ex-circus clown turned art dealer, Leo and Gertrude Stein saw the work of a then unknown Spanish painter, Pablo Picasso. Leo wished to purchase Picasso's painting of a nude girl holding a basket of red flowers, but Gertrude was opposed. According to her account in *The Autobiography of Alice B. Toklas*, she 'did not like the picture, she found something rather appalling in the drawing of the legs and feet, something that repelled and shocked her' (43). However, Leo prevailed, and the picture was purchased and hung in the atelier among the Cézannes and the Matisses.[34] Despite her initial shock, Stein was soon an admirer of Picasso's work; unlike Leo, she never wavered in her admiration, even at the extremes of Picasso's daring creative enterprise. She understood, as Leo emphatically did not, the significance and value of Picasso's later experiments in representation, culminating in his development of cubism.

Stein's first encounter with the painter himself was no less shocking than her first exposure to his work, but she recollects that her response to the man was more immediately positive than her response to the painting had been. Shortly after the purchase of *Young Girl with Basket of Flowers*, the Steins invited Picasso and his mistress Fernande to dinner. Stein describes this first meeting in *The Autobiography of Alice B. Toklas*:

> He was thin dark, alive with big pools of eyes and a violent but not rough way. He was sitting next to Gertrude Stein at dinner and she took up a piece of bread. This, said Picasso, snatching it back with violence, this piece of bread is mine. She laughed and he looked sheepish. That was the beginning of their intimacy.
>
> That evening Gertrude Stein's brother took out portfolio after portfolio of japanese prints to show Picasso, Gertrude Stein's brother was fond of japanese prints. Picasso solemnly and obediently looked at print after print and listened to the descriptions. He said under his breath to Gertrude Stein, he is very nice, your brother, but like all americans . . . he shows you japanese prints. Moi j'aime pas ça, no I don't care for it. As I [Alice Toklas] say Gertrude Stein and Pablo Picasso immediately understood each other. (46)

Like his painting, Picasso's behaviour at table is appalling, even violent. Nevertheless, Gertrude Stein is amused; his violence is no bar to intimacy. They finish the evening by understanding each other. Stein's rendering of this evening suggests that their understanding was considerably enhanced by Picasso's whispered response to Leo's æsthetic pronouncements.

In her various retrospective portrayals of her friendship with Picasso, Stein is at pains to insist on the symbiosis between herself and the painter. She characterizes their intimacy as inevitable and enduring. She proposes to explain their bond by the theory that Spain and America 'have something in common' (p 44). 'Gertrude Stein and spaniards are natural friends', Stein announces in the *Autobiography of Alice B. Toklas* (125). 'She [Gertrude Stein] always says that americans can understand spaniards. That they are the only two western nations that can realise abstraction. . . . Americans, so Gertrude Stein says, are like Spaniards, they are abstract and cruel' (91). The affinities between Spaniards and Americans, which Stein insists on, may seem far-fetched, but they served to establish a kind of familial connection between these otherwise unrelated individuals – Gertrude Stein and Pablo Picasso – a bond as strong and instinctual as that one might have with a brother.

Stein's written analyses of Picasso's character, both at the time she first knew him and subsequently during their long friendship, suggest coincidences in their very natures. For example, in *Picasso*, a 1938 appreciation of the painter and his work, Stein writes: 'He never enjoyed travelling, he always went where others already were, Picasso never had the pleasure of initiative. As he used to say of himself, he has a weak character and he allowed others to make decisions, that is the way it is, it was enough that he should do his work, decisions are never important, why make them' (61). Though writing about Picasso here, Stein echoes earlier self-descriptive passages from her autobiographical writing, thereby emphasising the affinity between her personality and Picasso's.

Shortly before meeting Picasso, Stein had begun working on *Three Lives*. Unlike the aborted *Making of Americans* and the hidden *Q.E.D.*, *Three Lives* was a work that Stein completed and saw through to publication. She was able to do so in part because of her friendship with Picasso. Although it is doubtful that she actually showed her work to him, she did discuss with him her ideas about writing as he did his about art. In Picasso she found someone passionately committed to a vital work of his own who treated her as an equal and who listened to her with respect and sympathy.[35] In *The Autobiography of Alice B. Toklas*, Stein conveys the reciprocity in the friendship between herself and the painter:

> She [Gertrude Stein] understands very well the basis of creation and therefore her advice and criticism is invaluable to all her friends. How often have I [Alice Toklas] heard Picasso say to her when she has said something about a picture of his and then illustrated by something she was trying to do, racontez-moi cela. In other words tell me about it. These two even to-day have long solitary conversations. They sit in two little low chairs up in his apartment studio, knee to knee and Picasso says, expliquez-moi cela. And they explain to each other. (77)

Stein has juxtaposed this anecdote to a glancing reference to Ernest Hemingway as one of 'the young' who 'when they have learnt all they can learn accuse her of an inordinate pride'. She acknowledges the truth of the accusation and declares that her pride comes from her realization that 'in english literature in her time she is the only one. She has always known it and now she says it' (77). When she began to work steadily and productively at her writing and when she began to know the value of what she was doing, she could sit 'knee to knee' with Picasso and say what she knew. Unlike lesser men (the young Hemingway, for instance, and perhaps her brother Leo as well), Picasso was not threatened by his need for explanations or by Stein's ability to supply them.

The pride which is so evident in her autobiographical writing was in short supply in 1905, however. Self-doubt was a more frequent midnight visitor to the study at rue de Fleurus than self-confidence. Just as the friendship with Picasso could accommodate her increasing mastery and confidence, so it could sustain her in periods of doubt.

She thought of herself and Picasso as having parallel work lives, a notion most vividly illustrated by her version of his creation of *Portrait of Gertrude Stein* in the winter of 1905–1906. According to Stein, she sat some eighty or ninety times for this portrait, and it was while walking across Paris to and from these sittings that she worked out in her head the story of 'Melanctha', the third and most experimental of the stories in *Three Lives*.[36] She sums up the results of their winter's work in *The Autobiography of Alice B. Toklas*:

> It had been a fruitful winter. In the long struggle with the portrait of Gertrude Stein, Picasso passed from the Harlequin, the charming early italian period to the intensive struggle which was to end in cubism. Gertrude Stein had written the story of Melanctha the negress, the second story of Three Lives which was the first definite step away from the nineteenth century and into the twentieth century in literature. (54)

In Picasso's struggle to express his vision of her, she saw an analogue to her own creative efforts. She presents the winter of 1905-1906 as a pivotal moment in both careers, though in fact art historians do not find Picasso's painting of Gertrude Stein's portrait as critical a moment in his development as Stein believed it to be.[37]

As for the portrait itself, she reports that others found it unsatisfactory, bearing little or no resemblance to its subject. The painter and the model, however, 'were content' (ABT 57). In writing of their shared response to the portrait, Stein emphasises their solidarity in the face of the world's opinion. Indeed, she often portrays the two of them set apart from the company in which they find themselves, having whispered conversations in which they share viewpoints not understood by the others. Here is one such representation from *The Autobiography of Alice B. Toklas*:

Picasso and Gertrude Stein stood together talking. I [Alice Toklas] stood back and looked [at the paintings]. . . . I heard Gertrude Stein say, and mine. Picasso thereupon brought out a smaller picture, a rather unfinished thing that could not finish, very pale almost white, two figures, they were all there but very unfinished and not finishable. Picasso said, but he will never accept it. Yes, I know, answered Gertrude Stein. But just the same it is the only one in which it is all there. Yes, I know, he replied and they fell silent. (22)

Though Stein does not identify the 'he' who 'will never accept it', one suspects that she is referring to her brother.

This passage implies what Stein elsewhere states – that she was 'alone at this time in understanding him [Picasso]'. She understood him because she was 'expressing the same thing in literature' that he was in painting (P 42). In fact, however, Stein was not alone in understanding Picasso. Early in his career, he had a good number of friends, patrons and followers, and in a remarkably short time, as art careers go, he was a financial and critical success.[38] What accounts for Stein's misreading of Picasso's career? It is likely that she imagined herself and Picasso together against the rest of the world because she needed an ally in her own opposition to and eventual liberation from her brother's domination. It was not in the world at large so much as in the Stein household that Gertrude Stein was alone in understanding Picasso. It was not the world that misunderstood and rejected Picasso's work; it was Leo Stein. At the same time, he also misunderstood and rejected Stein's work. In a 1905 letter to Mabel Weeks, Stein reports having shown *Three Lives* to Leo:

> I am afraid that I can never write the great American novel. . . . Leo he said there wasn't no art in Lovett's book and then he was bad and wouldn't tell me that there was in mine so I went to bed very missable but I don't care. . . . Dey [the three stories] is very simple and very vulgar and I don't think they will interest the great American public. I am very sad Mamie. [Lovett was a mutual friend from Harvard.]39

On this particular evening, Leo seems to have favoured silence to outright criticism, but his later comments about his sister's writing give the flavour of his negative response to her work and show that he saw, as she did, the connection between Picasso's painting and her writing, a connection he deplored. In a 1913 letter to the same Mabel Weeks to whom Gertrude had earlier written, he explained how he and Gertrude had come to be estranged:

> It was of course a serious thing for her [Gertrude] that I can't abide her stuff and think it abominable. . . . To this has been added my utter refusal to accept the later phases of Picasso with whose tendency Gertrude has so closely allied herself. They both seem to me entirely on the wrong track.
> Picasso . . . wants to be the creator of a great and original form. . . . Her artistic capacity is, I think, extremely small. I have just been looking over the Melanctha thing again. Gertrude's mind is about as little nimble as a mind can be. . . . Well, Gertrude also wants to create a great

and original form. . . .   Both he [Picasso] and Gertrude
are using their intellects, which they ain't got, to do what
would need the finest critical tact, which they ain't got
neither, and they are in my belief turning out the most
Godalmighty rubbish that is to be found.[40]

His estimation of Stein's work (and of cubism) was never
to vary. He wrote parodies of her writing which he sent
to friends and showed to her. He called her stupid in any
number of letters to their friends, letters in which he deni-
grated her work which he described variously as nonsense,
tommyrot, bosh, rubbish, an abomination, foolishness, and
so forth. What prompted the venom of these attacks was
probably his own inability first to paint and then to write,
a creative block that he would discuss at length in the same
letters in which he was tearing his sister apart.

Shari Benstock has written that Picasso served as a
'substitute brother' for Stein;[41] I believe he served more as
an alter ego than as a brother. The last thing Stein needed
was another brother. She did, however, need someone on
whom to model herself as she broke free from her brother's
influence. Since asserting her independence from Leo
entailed rejection and isolation, she found an ally whom
she imagined as being similarly isolated and rejected. She
admired the fact that Picasso persevered, that he continued
working no matter how the public – or Leo – responded
to his work. She found this tenacity heroic. And Gertrude
Stein did want to be a hero. So, with Picasso as a model
and a mentor, she continued to write her way through the
nights at rue de Fleurus while she continued to live with
her brother and his criticism.

V

By 1907, when Gertrude Stein met Alice Toklas, her
intimacy with Leo had been stretched thinly between the

poles of their opposing egos. In *Everybody's Autobiography*, Stein tells how 'gradually' and 'slowly' the two who had always been 'together' 'little by little . . . never met again'. The trouble, as Stein explains it, was that 'gradually [she] was writing' and 'slowly [she] was knowing that [she] was a genius'. She writes that at first she did not show what she was writing to her brother. Then he looked at what she was writing and said nothing about it. However, 'gradually he had something to say about it'. What he said was that her work was not art, but merely self-expression without intrinsic artistic merit. She claims not to have listened to his criticism; she claims that it 'did not trouble' her; she claims that she 'knew it was not true'. But she also claims, 'It destroyed him for me and it destroyed me for him' (58–60). After all, as she explains, Leo was supposed to have been the genius in the family. She writes:

> That is the way he felt about it and it was a natural thing because he understood everything and if you understand everything and besides that are leading and besides that do do what you do, there is no reason why it should not be. . . .   The only thing about it was that it was I who was the genius. There was no reason for it but I was, and he was not . . . and that was the beginning of the ending and we always had been together and now we were never at all together. (61)

Into the void created by the destruction of the intimacy between Leo and Gertrude stepped Alice B. Toklas – thirty-one years old, unmarried, and eager to begin an expatriate life away from the domestic burden of keeping house for her father and her younger brother whom she had raised after her mother's death in 1897. On a September afternoon in 1907, newly arrived in Paris from San Francisco and accompanied by her friend and travelling companion, Harriet Levy, Alice Toklas paid a visit to the home of Harriet's friends, Michael and Sarah Stein. There Alice met Michael's younger sister, Gertrude. Alice describes the meeting in her autobiography:

> In the room were Mr. and Mrs. Stein and Gertrude Stein . . . who held my complete attention, as she did for all the many years I knew her until her death, and all these empty ones since then. She was a golden brown presence, burned by the Tuscan sun and with a golden glint in her warm brown hair. She was dressed in a warm brown corduroy suit. She wore a large round coral brooch and when she talked . . . I thought her voice came from this brooch. It was unlike anyone else's voice – deep, full, velvety like a great contralto's, like two voices. She was large and heavy with delicate small hands and a beautifully modeled and unique head.[42]

Alice Toklas became no less central to Gertrude Stein's life than Stein was to hers. Stein began almost immediately to court her, inviting her to rue de Fleurus, arranging for her and Harriet to have French lessons from Picasso's mistress, securing quarters for Alice and Harriet close to rue de Fleurus, introducing them to the new art and the artists, and taking long walks about Paris with Alice.

Stein had begun working on *The Making of Americans* again, and she showed it to Alice who recalls her response: 'It was very exciting, more exciting than anything else had ever been. Even, I said to her laughing, more exciting than Picasso's pictures promise to be'.[43] Toklas's praise and understanding were just the balm Stein's bruised pride needed in the face of her brother's rejection, and the friendship went forward through the winter of 1907–1908. In the summer of 1908, Alice and Harriet rented a small house near the Steins' summer villa in Fiesole; during this summer of memorable walks in the Tuscan hills the intimacy between Gertrude and Alice deepened, though it was probably not until spring 1909 that they became lovers. During the winter of 1908–1909, Gertrude nicknamed Alice the 'old maid mermaid', suggesting perhaps a sexual reticence on Alice's part. By spring however, as Alice coyly explains in her autobiography, 'The old maid mermaid had gone into oblivion and I had been gathering wild violets'.[44]

Also at this time Alice began to make herself indispensable to Gertrude. She taught herself to type, and she came every day to rue de Fleurus to type the pages of *The Making of Americans* which Gertrude had written during the night. Gertrude would join Alice at lunchtime, and the two would spend the afternoon and evening together. When *Three Lives* appeared in 1909, Alice helped distribute copies and subscribed to a clipping service so that she could keep Gertrude apprised of the book's reception. Every Sunday, the cook's night off, Alice came to the atelier and cooked an American dinner for Leo and Gertrude.

When Harriet Levy returned to San Francisco in 1910, Alice moved into a small room in the rue de Fleurus apartment. Leo seems to have welcomed her presence since she acted as a buffer between him and Gertrude, the two of whom were growing ever more estranged. In a 1913 letter, Leo wrote: 'As we [he and Gertrude] have come to maturity, we have come to find that there is practically nothing under the heavens that we don't either disagree about, or at least regard with different sympathies'.[45] Between 1905 and 1913 Stein had found her voice, first as a writer and then as a 'disagreeable' sister. She was no longer the quiet, smiling, dark presence in Leo Stein's salon. (Ironically, as she became more outspoken, he became increasingly hard of hearing, his deafness an uncanny physical manifestation of his inability to listen to others.) In 1913, then, Gertrude and Leo divided their art, Gertrude keeping the Picassos and Leo taking the Renoirs, the two sharing, after some squabbling, the Matisses and

the Cézannes, and Leo left rue de Fleurus to settle in
Settignano, near Florence, where he lived until his death
in 1947.

That left Gertrude and Alice in command at rue de
Fleurus though there has been considerable debate about
who exactly was in command in the Stein/Toklas ménage.
In *Everybody's Autobiography*, Stein provides an amusing
glimpse of the 'arrangement' between the two. She is
recounting the story of a photo session in their Chicago
hotel room during her 1934 tour of the United States. She
asks the photographer what a 'layout' is. He responds:

> It is four or five pictures of you doing anything. All right
> I said what do you want me to do. Why he said there is
> your airplane bag suppose you unpack it, oh I said Miss
> Toklas always does that oh no I could not do that, well he
> said there is the telephone suppose you telephone well I
> said yes but I never do Miss Toklas always does that,
> well he said what can you do, well I said I can put my
> hat on and take my hat off and I can put my coat on
> and I can take it off and I like water I can drink a glass
> of water all right he said do that so I did that. (188–9)

It is certainly clear from every account of the couple that
Toklas took complete care of Stein. She cooked, cleaned
and managed the house; she took care of social and business
affairs, edited, typed and even published Stein's work, and
nurtured her reputation. She saw to it that Stein was never
bothered by anything or anyone. In short, she was the
perfect 'wife', and from Stein's writing (in which erotic
and domestic details are freely included), it is obvious that
Gertrude thought of herself as a husband. Their assump-
tion of traditional roles has caused some consternation
among feminist critics who see Stein as reproducing in
her own relationship the patterns of oppression inherent
in the patriarchal marriage 'story'.[46] However, I agree with

Catharine Stimpson that 'to oversimplify the Stein/Toklas marriage and ménage is stupid'. If Stein did, as Stimpson says, 'claim the prerogatives of the male,' she was, again in Stimpson's words, 'a good husband'.[47] The fact is that the marriage was satisfying to both and not because Toklas effaced herself so that Stein could do to Toklas what Leo had done to Gertrude. Toklas's voice was as strong as Stein's; her will perhaps stronger. But when it came to Stein's writing, Toklas believed that Stein was a 'genius', and she was willing to do whatever was necessary to foster and protect Stein's talents. In return, she was central to Stein's life and to her art, a position that seems to have pleased her. Some look into their lovers' eyes to see themselves reflected in the other, but Toklas had only to look at the words she typed every day of her married life. In that half of Stein's life in which she made what she made, the half we are about to enter, Alice Toklas is everywhere, inscribed in every text that Stein made as she sat in the comfort of the home that Alice created for her.

2 Gertrude Stein's Writing/Gertrude Stein's Writing

I

At first glance, the title of this chapter seems to repeat itself, and my reader may conclude that I have acquired a habit of repetition from my subject, the writer whose signature phrase is 'rose is a rose is a rose'. However, with my phrase 'Gertrude Stein's writing', I mean to suggest two very different kinds of writing and two very different ways of looking at Gertrude Stein's writing, and so I have said the same thing twice – or have I? Looked at one way, 'Stein's writing' is a possessive noun and a gerund, and looked at in that way, Stein's writing is a static literary product which will stay put while we analyse it in terms of style and content, structure and meaning, intention and excecution. Looked at another way, 'Stein's writing' is a contraction of a subject and a helping verb followed by the present participle of the verb 'to write', and it means 'Stein is writing'. In that way of looking, you are asked to shift your attention from the product to the process of making that product. In this and the next chapter, then, we will look at Gertrude Stein's writing, and we will also see Gertrude Stein writing.

Stein herself identified two primary modes of composition: writing 'what you intended to write' and writing 'what you are writing' (FIA 122–4). The two works written between 1903 and 1911 that we will consider in chapters 2 and 3, *Three Lives* and *The Making of Americans*, enact and record Stein's shift from the first mode to the second. To write according to one's intention is to have a plan for the writing (probably one modelled on other pre-existing plans, 'what has always been intended, by any one, to be written' [FIA 124]); this kind of writing requires that the writer set limits and goals so that the writer's intention can be realized and the reader's expectations met. To write what you are writing without intention, on the other hand, is to make writing into a process of discovery;[1] it requires nothing except that the writer continue writing. This writing is open-ended (not finished and not finishable, as Stein said of one of Picasso's paintings) and its meaning is indeterminate.[2]

When Stein began *Three Lives* and *The Making of Americans*, she intended to represent characters, to report events in their lives and to recreate a remembered reality. She intended to effect a correspondence between her words and extralinguistic objects, qualities and actions.[3] However, in the process of fulfilling her intention, she discovered that language could do other things besides name, describe and report. It could, for instance, embody rhythms – the rhythm of personality, of conversation, of human action and interaction. (Later she was to say that writing could keep time with the rhythm of a dog lapping water from a bowl or of traffic passing on the street.) If freed from intention and expectation (and eventually from grammatical and rhetorical constraints), language could also play, and the artist whose medium was language could play with words or could examine and ponder them as objects in a composition. At this extreme, literature would no longer be about an extralinguistic situation; it would be about the materials and processes of its own construction. In Stein's work, then, the objective world becomes less and less important, and the object that is the work of art and the process by which it is created become paramount. The works we will examine in this chapter mark the beginning of Stein's lifelong questioning of the representational function of art and of the signifying function of language in literary texts.

II

Written between 1905 and 1906, *Three Lives* consists of three novellas: 'The Good Anna', 'The Gentle Lena' and 'Melanctha: Each One As She May'.[4] They are the fictional life histories of the three working-class women named in their titles. Anna and Lena are German immigrants who work as servants; Melanctha is an American black woman who has no regular employment but who acts as a kind of servant to her friends and to the various women she rooms with. Like Anna and Lena, Melanctha is 'always ready to do things for people' (99); all three women are routinely victimized because of their essential passivity and emotional dependence. Even the bossy Anna and the adventurous Melanctha exhibit, like the more docile Lena, a kind of servitude of the heart.

The good Anna Federner, who was modelled on Leo and Gertrude's Baltimore housekeeper, is a servant all her adult life, and we follow her from her first position in Germany to America where she has a succession of posts. Her first American mistress is Miss Mary Wadsmith, a widow with a son and a daughter; Anna has this position for many years but finally gives it up when the daughter, Jane, marries, sets up her own house and invites her mother and Anna to live with her. Anna cannot tolerate any interference with her management of the household, and she realizes that in Jane's house she will be subject to Jane's will. Anna prefers to work for 'lazy, careless or all helpless' women or for men, so that 'the burden of their lives could fall on [her]' (22). Anna next works for a bachelor doctor until he gets married and then she settles with her 'beloved Miss Mathilda', a character much like Stein herself, with whom Anna remains until Miss Mathilda moves to Europe. Anna has two close friends, Mrs. Lehntman, a widow with two children who runs a home for unwed mothers, and Mrs. Drehten, an overworked mother of seven with an alcoholic husband. To these friends, Anna gives all of her hard-earned savings and what little free time she has, carrying the burden of their lives as she carries the domestic burdens of her employers. Her only pleasure that does not wear her out at the same time that it pleases her comes from her dogs – Rags, Peter and Baby. Anna finishes her life running a boarding house for young gentlemen. She does not charge enough money to enable her to hire help and so must do all the work herself. Although the cause of her death is presumably cancer, she actually seems to have worked herself to death.

Lena Mainz, the gentle Lena of the second story, dies in childbirth, but she too seems to have been worn out long before her death. Brought from Germany by her aunt, Mrs. Haydon, she is first placed in service and then married off to Herman Kreder, the son of a German tailor, a marriage engineered by Mrs. Haydon and Mr. and Mrs. Kreder; neither Lena nor Herman 'care much to get married' (228). From the minute she enters the house of her in-laws, Lena is under the control of her tyrannical mother-in-law who tortures her with scolding and criticism. From her first pregnancy to her fourth and fatal one, Lena becomes increasingly 'careless', 'dazed' and 'lifeless' (251). When she dies 'nobody knew just how it had happened to her' (253); it seems as though the life had been leaking out of her in a gentle whisper over the years and no one had listened closely enough to hear her expire.

Unlike Anna who is a spinster and Lena who submits unenthusiastically to the performance of her marital duties, Melanctha has a sexual self which Stein develops fully, if euphemistically, by depicting Melanctha's sexual awakening in adolescence, her 'wandering after wisdom' where men work in the freightyards, docks and construction sites of the city, and her sexual initiation by Jane Harden, a hard-drinking, rough, but intelligent woman, who becomes Melanctha's mentor for a time.[5] The centerpiece of the story is Melanctha's affair with Jeff Campbell, the young doctor who tends Melanctha's mother in her final illness. This affair is the centerpiece insofar as it occupies the largest chunk of the narrative, though it seems to mean less to Melanctha than her subsequent friendship with Rose Johnson and engagement to Jem Richards. Stein invests narrative energy in the affair between Jeff and Melanctha partly because it is the transposition of the affair between Adele and Helen depicted in the earlier novel *Q.E.D.* Many of the passages in 'Melanctha' correspond to passages in the earlier book. Stein is once again trying to work through the dynamics of her relationship with May Bookstaver by pairing the cautious and repressed Jeff with the sexually experienced and wanton Melanctha. The affair is doomed because the lovers are at cross-purposes. When Melanctha pursues Jeff, he resists her; when he gives in to his feelings for her, he cannot help but retain some of his former resistance to her; this drives her away, so that when he is finally completely in love with her, she is no longer interested in him. Similarly, the friendship with Rose Johnson and the affair with Jem Richards end in estrangement and loss for Melanctha, who, like Lena and Anna, dies an understated, off-stage death, having already been effectively removed from the life of the narrative.

Three Lives not only tells the three stories I have just outlined, but it also tells the story of Gertrude Stein's changing æsthetic, and it is this latter story that will now occupy us. We will trace Stein's increasing interest in writing as process rather than product, and we will see how she eventually came to focus in her fiction on the process of composition to the exclusion of all other events.

Just before Stein began *Three Lives*, Leo had urged her to read Flaubert and had given her a copy of *Trois Contes*, suggesting that she translate it if she wanted to learn something about narrative. 'The Good Anna' shows that she at least went so far as to read the first of Flaubert's three stories, 'Un coeur simple', whose central character, Félicité, is a simple, uneducated and devoted servant. Flaubert's story undoubtedly influenced Stein's decision to write about uneducated, working-class women when she had before drawn characters of her own class and background in *Q.E.D.*, *Fernhurst* and the early fragment of *The Making of Americans*. There are also a few superficial echoes of 'Un coeur simple' in 'The Good Anna'. The most interesting of these echoes are the parrots that both Félicité and Anna have as pets.

Whereas in Flaubert's story the parrot is a memorable emblem of the servant's pathetic loneliness and isolation, a remarkable device that evokes sympathy for Félicité at the same time that its ironic presentation tempers the very sympathy it evokes, in Stein's story the parrot, a peace-offering from Jane, is reduced to a minor detail. After its introduction we hear nothing about it until Anna goes to live with Miss Mathilda, who does not like the parrot's scream. With no hesitation Anna gives the parrot 'to the Drehten girls to keep' (56), and we hear the last of it from the narrator who informs us that 'the parrot had passed out of Anna's life. She had really never loved the parrot and now she hardly thought to ask for him, even when she visited the Drehtens' (62–3). Thus, Stein demotes Flaubert's invention and rejects the literariness of his portentous parrot. In so doing, she points to Flaubert's precedence but, at the same time, dismisses his influence – and by extension her brother's.

The parrot is merely a sign, however, of a much more substantial divergence in *Three Lives* from the Flaubertian model. In 'The Good Anna' the difference is already apparent, and the difference spreads as Stein proceeds. 'Un coeur simple' is as much about a place as it is about a person. Set in Flaubert's native province where he spent his summer holidays as a boy, the story is touched by a nostaliga for times past, tempered, however, by the dispassionate narration and the frequent irony. Flaubert's interest in place is apparent in the carefully detailed settings and in the representation of the community of people Flaubert remembered as having inhabited these places. Thus, 'Un coeur simple' opens with references to farms that actually belonged to the Flauberts and offers the reader a long description of the house of Félicité's mistress before describing Félicité herself. The house is given to us in detail, the decor so specific that we know the style of the furniture, the pattern of the wallpaper and the artist responsible for the etchings on the wall. These objective details resonate; they are emblematic in the sense that they are meant to convey information about characters and about narrative point of view. In fact, one could say that the portrait of Félicité evolves out of such textual details. Stein, too, sets her story in a place she has inhabited – the Bridgepoint of *Three Lives* is Baltimore – but aside from some references to the south and to warm weather, the stories could be taking place anywhere in the United States, so little interest has Stein in conveying a sense of place. Stein does offer a description of Miss Mathilda's house:

It was a funny little house, one of a whole row of all the same kind that made a close pile like a row of dominoes that a child knocks over, for they were built along a street which at this point came down a steep hill. They were funny little houses, two stories high, with red brick fronts and long white steps. (9)

Just as this description keeps us outside the house, so too does it keep us outside the story. Stein's descriptions (when she provides them) do not generate meaning as Flaubert's do. Her objects are not keys that open doors to the heart of her story.

Once we are taken inside Miss Mathilda's house, visual description drops away. This house is furnished only with Anna's voice – 'This one little house was always very full with . . . Anna's voice that scolded, managed, grumbled all day long' (9) – and Stein immediately gives us a sample of the scolding and grumbling to which Anna subjects the dogs, the underservants and even Miss Mathilda. Stein's ear for the cadences and syntax of immigrant speech is exceptional, and Anna comes alive for us through her own words. Anna spends her life trying to get people to do what's right by scolding and instructing (much of which we hear directly), and the climaxes of the narrative come when Anna must deliver herself of important speeches. In contrast, Flaubert's Félicité hardly ever speaks, and her story is almost entirely narrated in the dispassionate voice of an omniscient third person. It is in its focus on the speech of the central character that 'The Good Anna' differs most markedly from 'Un coeur simple'. One can say that in Stein's fiction, speech replaces description and report as the primary mode of authorial communication.

This interest in speech increases as Stein works her way through the second story of the trio. In 'The Gentle Lena', it is not the voice of the central character that we hear, but the voices of the people who surround her – her friends, her fellow servants, her aunt, and finally her mother-in-law, who almost scolds her to death. Lena is herself very quiet and abstracted; the narrator describes her as 'dreamy' and 'not there' (222). She always does as she is told, whether she wants to or not. If she has opinions or feelings, she does not express them, in part because of her acquiescent nature, but also because Stein never gives her a voice. Instead, we are made to feel the weight of the words of others upon her. Like Lena, the narrator herself seems overwhelmed by the talk of the other characters. That is, the narrative voice is increasingly absorbed by the voices of Mrs. Haydon, the Kreders and others.

In 'The Good Anna' the narrative voice is distinct from the voice of the characters. The narrator introduces speeches and comments upon them in ways that interpret them for the reader. For example, before an impending confrontation between Anna and Jane, the narrator describes Anna:

> She had stopped just within the door, her body and her face stiff with repression, her teeth closed hard and the white lights flashing sharply in the pale, clean blue of her eyes. Her bearing was full of the strange coquetry of anger and of fear, the stiffness, the bridling, the suggestive movement underneath the rigidity of forced control, all the queer ways the passions have to show themselves all one. (25-6)

Then Anna speaks:

> 'Miss Mary, I can't stand it any more like this. When you tell me anything to do, I do it. I do everything I can and you know I work myself sick for you. The blue dressings in your room makes too much work to have for summer. Miss Jane don't know what work is. If you want to do things like that I go away'. (26)

The narrator follows with an analysis of Anna's speech and its effect on Miss Mary:

> Her words had not the strength of meaning they were meant to have, but the power in the mood of Anna's soul frightened and awed Miss Mary through and through. (26)

The narrator's vocabulary is more sophisticated than the character's; her grammar is correct, her syntax complex but standard. An outsider, she observes Anna speaking and presents the event as a picture. In contrast, Anna uses simple words, relies on colloquial commonplaces, makes grammatical errors and speaks a kind of 'broken' English. She is inside her own anger and expressing it.

In 'The Gentle Lena' Stein begins with the same narrative convention: the narrator speaks with one voice, the characters with another. In the following exchange between Lena and her friend, Mary, we have no trouble distinguishing the narrator's voice from the voices of the characters:

> 'What you got on your finger Lena,' Mary, one of the girls she always sat with, one day asked her. Mary was good natured, quick, intelligent and Irish.
>
> Lena had just picked up the fancy paper made accordion that the little girl had dropped beside her, and was making it squeak sadly as she pulled it with her brown, strong, awkward finger.
>
> 'Why, what is it, Mary, paint?' said Lena, putting her finger to her mouth to taste the dirt spot.
>
> 'That's awful poison Lena, don't you know?' said Mary, 'that green paint that you just tasted.'
>
> Lena had sucked a good deal of the green paint from her finger. She stopped and looked hard at the finger. She did not know just how much Mary meant by what she said.
>
> 'Ain't it poison, Nellie, that green paint, that Lena sucked just now,' said Mary. 'Sure it is Lena, it's real poison, I ain't foolin' this time anyhow.' (219)

Although the distinction here between the voices of the narrator and of the characters is clear, the narrator's vocabulary and point of view in 'The Gentle Lena' are closer to those of the characters than they were in 'The Good Anna'. This narrator seems no more educated or intelligent than the people whose story she tells; her language abilities seem only slightly better than theirs (and consequently, her analyses and interpretations seem less reliable). As the story proceeds, the voice distinctions increasingly blur and often disappear altogether. Compare the following examples of the mix of narration, indirect discourse and direct discourse:

(1) The conventional though limited narrator is distinct from the character:

> Mrs. Haydon spoke to Lena very often about Herman. Mrs. Haydon sometimes got very angry with Lena. She was afraid that Lena, for once, was going to be stubborn, now when it was all fixed right for her to be married. . . .
>
> 'Why don't you answer with some sense, Lena, when I ask you if you don't like Herman Kreder. You stand there so stupid and don't answer just like you ain't heard a word what I been saying to you. I never see anybody like you, Lena.' (229)

(2) The voice of the narrator blurs with that of the characters, and the indirect discourse reported by the narrator echoes and merges with the direct discourse of the characters:

> Mrs. Haydon was very angry with poor Lena when she saw her. She scolded her hard because she was so foolish, and now Herman had gone off and nobody could tell where he had gone to, and all because *Lena always . . . stood there so stupid and did not answer what anybody asked her.* . . . Did Lena think it gave Mrs. Haydon any pleasure, to work so hard to make Lena happy, and get her a good husband, and then Lena

was so thankless and never did anything that anybody wanted. It was a lesson to poor Mrs. Haydon not to do things any more for anybody. . . . *It just made trouble for her and her husband did not like it. He always said she was too good, and nobody ever thanked her for it, and there Lena was always standing stupid and not answering anything anybody wanted.* . . . [Direct discourse now begins.] '*No, it ain't no use your standin' there and cryin'*, now, Lena. It's too late now to care about that Herman. You should have cared some before, and then you wouldn't have to stand and cry now, and be a disappointment to me, and then *I get scolded by my husband for taking care of everybody, and nobody ever thankful.* I am glad you got the sense to feel sorry now, Lena, anyway, and I try to do what I can to help you out in your trouble, only you don't deserve to have anybody take any trouble for you.'

(232–3) (emphasis added)

The effect of Stein's increasing use of the second mode of narration is to fill the reader's 'ear' with talk and to deny us the relief and distancing normally provided by the narrative voice. Like the mesmerized and unresisting Lena, we are inundated by all this talk which bubbles out of the narrative like so much lava, picking up momentum as it goes.

This tendency to foreground conversation is carried to an extreme in 'Melanctha'. Here, not only does Stein merge direct and indirect discourse and blur the distinction between narrator and characters, but she also allows talk to practically obliterate narrative. 'Melanctha' is not about Melanctha Herbert in the same way that 'The Good Anna' is about Anna Federner or that 'The Gentle Lena' is about Lena Mainz. The lives of the latter two women are narrated as a sequence of events revealed to the reader at fairly regular intervals. The narrative of Melanctha's life, on the other hand, is a narrow frame around the edges

of the composition, and there are long stretches of prose
during which a reader may lose sight completely of the
story line. The text begins near the end of Melanctha's
life, with Melanctha helping her friend Rose Johnson give
birth to and take care of her baby until it dies shortly after
its birth. The narrative then takes us back to Melanctha's
childhood and through her young adulthood, bringing
us up to the moment when she meets Jeff Campbell.
These events occupy one-sixth of the text. Toward the
end of 'Melanctha', Rose Johnson is reintroduced; in the
remaining one-sixth of the composition, we hear of how she
and Melanctha met, and we are once again taken through
the birth and death of Rose's baby and quickly through
subsequent events leading to Melanctha's early death from
consumption. Thus, fully two-thirds of 'Melanctha' is given
over to something other than a narration of the events of
Melanctha's life. That something is talk – the seemingly
endless conversations between Melanctha and Jeff. (Even
in the narrative frame, conversation is foregrounded as it
had been in the earlier stories.) In a certain sense, we
can say that 'Melanctha' is about talking (and, implicitly,
about listening) since conversation is the event that most
often occurs in its pages. Moreover, since the characters
talk about talking and about listening, meaning, saying,
understanding, remembering, telling, thinking and asking,
we can say that 'Melanctha' is about language acts.

There are isolated lines in 'The Good Anna' and 'The
Gentle Lena' that could be said to prefigure the linguistic
theme of 'Melanctha'. For example, when Anna must tell
Miss Mary that she is not going to go with her to live
with Jane, her words leave Miss Mary 'puzzled'. 'She did
not understand what Anna meant by what she said' (31).
This is precisely the problem Jeff and Melanctha face.
Echoing the narrator of 'The Good Anna', Melanctha says
repeatedly to Jeff, 'I certainly don't understand what you
meant by what you was just saying', and Jeff to Melanctha,

'I certainly don't know for sure I know just all what you mean by what you are always saying to me'. Even though they endlessly say what they mean, they almost always fail to communicate. The problem lies as much with the listening as it does with the speaking. Melanctha listens to understand, Jeff to know. As Mary Field Belenky has pointed out in her study of women's ways of knowing, understanding involves intimacy and equality between self and object while knowledge implies separation from the object and mastery over it. Basing her discussion on Carol Gilligan's earlier influential work, *In a Different Voice*, Belenky distinguishes between 'really talking', in which the participants join together to arrive at a new understanding (a kind of talking that requires careful listening) and 'didactic talking', in which the speaker's intention is to hold forth, to impart knowledge.[6] To really talk means to reach into the experience of the other, as Melanctha did when she 'sat at Jane [Harden]'s feet for many hours . . . and felt Jane's wisdom'. Jane Harden taught Melanctha 'how to go the ways that lead to wisdom' (94). 'There was nothing good or bad in doing, feeling, thinking or in talking, that Jane spared her . . . and so slowly, but aways with increasing strength and feeling, Melanctha began to really understand' (96–7). For the didactic talker, talking is never about this kind of process of discovery and exploration. Jeff is a didactic talker when he meets Melanctha.[7] He 'always liked to talk to everybody . . . about his thinking about what he could do for the coloured people' (105–6). He is very sure he knows what he is talking about when he explains to Melanctha his belief that the proper behavior for his race is living quietly, avoiding excitement, 'working hard and caring about their working and living regular with their families and saving up all their money' (110). When Melanctha listens to him she tries to enter into his experience through his words as she had with Jane, but she finds a discrepancy between what he says and what

he does. He says he believes in religion for his people,
yet he does not go to church; he says he disapproves of
fast living, yet he admires Jane Harden and is her friend.
Melanctha cannot understand what he means if his words
do not correspond to his deeds.

She also has trouble understanding him because his
words are often disconnected from his feelings. For example, one evening early in the relationship, he and Melanctha
are sitting quietly together on the stairs in her mother's
house. Jeff begins to feel sexually attracted to Melanctha
and to wonder if she feels the same way. 'Slowly he felt
that surely they must both have this feeling. It was so
important that he knew that she must have it' (109).
Full of these feelings, he begins to speak – but not about
the feelings. He talks 'about how the lamp was smelling.
Jefferson began to explain what it is that makes a lamp get
to smelling. Melanctha let him talk. She did not answer, and
then he stopped in his talking. Soon Melanctha began to sit
up straighter and then she started in to question' (109). She
is not, however, interested in knowing about lamps. Since
her goal as a talker is to understand the other speaker, her
questions are aimed at the unexpressed feelings behind
Jeff's words. Again she seeks to enter his experience:

> You ain't a bit like good people Dr. Campbell, like the
> good people you are always saying are just like you. I
> know good people Dr. Campbell, and you ain't a bit
> like men who are good and got religion. You are just as
> free and easy as any man can be Dr. Campbell. . . . I
> certainly don't understand just what it is you mean by
> all that you was just saying to me. I know you mean
> honest Dr. Campbell, and I am always trying to believe
> you, but I can't say as I see just what you mean when
> you say you want to be good and real pious, because I
> am very certain Dr. Campbell that you ain't that kind
> of a man at all. (109)

Here she understands him better than she knows; as the reader can see, she has read his mind.

Jeff declares himself ready to learn about women, with Melanctha as his teacher. However, the more he struggles to understand ('he wanted very badly to be really understanding'), the less he knows. 'Jefferson always had thought he knew something about women. Now he found that really he knew nothing. He did not know the least bit about Melanctha' (118). In a sense, he has to give up the desire to know in order to understand. He must learn to give himself over to the process of making meaning and to the uncertainty which that process entails, and he must learn this through a long and painful struggle with language.

As a writer, Stein seems to have had a conversion similar to the one Jeff undergoes in 'Melanctha'.[8] As I pointed out earlier, Jeff and Melanctha correspond to the lovers Adele and Helen in *Q.E.D.* and to Stein and Bookstaver in life. In creating the autobiographical *Q.E.D.*, Stein was trying to determine what had gone wrong in her love affair. The title suggests that the text will be a formulation, a demonstration of a principle. The subtitle of 'Melanctha' – 'Each One As She May' – suggests a more tentative view of the world. Here there are no first principles, no demonstrations, no rules; characters muddle through as best they can – each as she may. In *Q.E.D.*, the characters and the narrator are articulate people who, when faced with the unruliness of the passions, use language to analyse behaviour, formulate experience and reach conclusions on which to base future action. Much as Jeff would like to accomplish the same feat in 'Melanctha', he cannot. He is swamped by the strength of his emotions, the inadequacy of his language and the inconclusiveness of his experience. In writing 'Melanctha', Stein makes no attempt to rise above the messiness of her characters' experience. Instead, she allows the writing to be as inconclusive and disorienting as the experience it records.[9] In short, 'Melanctha' is a model of Stein's own activity as a writer. It must also be a model of our activity as readers. We cannot reduce the process of Jeff and Melanctha's relationship to a single meaning or even to a simple resolution. Our understanding of it must evolve from an immersion in its process, and our understanding will always be provisional. Each one of us will make meaning of this process as she may.

The fixed meaning of Jeff and Melanctha's experience is difficult to come by because the words through which we might explain and know that experience are slippery commodities. Their meanings depend entirely on context and point of view – in other words, on where they appear in the process of making meaning. Stein demonstrates this chameleon-like quality of language through the use of repetition. The more she repeats a word or a phrase, the more she reveals its unreliability. Take, for example, the adjective 'good'. The prose in *Three Lives* is exceedingly dependent on adjectives. Epithets and adjective strings abound: 'pretty, cheerful Lizzy', 'melancholy Molly' (12) and 'rough old Katy' (15); 'she [Melanctha] was patient, submissive, soothing, and untiring, while the sullen, childish, cowardly, black Rosie grumbled' (77). The most often repeated adjectives are value words like 'good' (also 'right', 'decent', 'regular', 'careless', 'bad', and so forth). What the repetitions tell us is that the quality (cheerfulness, laziness, goodness) is constant. Lizzy is always cheerful; Miss Mathilda is always lazy; Anna is always good. Yet we are never sure what it means to be good, nor are we sure whether it is good to be good. In a text in which the reader is forced to rely on adjectives for information, adjectives are shown to be unreliable. While goodness persists (is repeated and insisted on), its meaning is always changing.

Anna is 'good' in that she works very hard, saves her money and sacrifices herself (and her money) for others. In every situation she behaves the same way, and the narrator calls that way 'good'. Yet, as her doctor finds, it is difficult to 'persuade even a good Anna to do things that were for her own good' (28). Anna's goodness is bad for Anna. Moreover, her goodness often supports the badness of others; her sacrifices allow others to be lazy, careless and indifferent.

The word 'good' is also applied to people whose goodness is questionable. When Mrs. Lehntman is first introduced she is labelled 'pleasant, magnetic, efficient and good' (27). Later the narrator tells us that she is 'good and honest' (47). However, Mrs. Lehntman takes advantage of Anna, borrowing and never repaying Anna's life savings to buy a larger house for her unwed mothers. Even though the house is too expensive, Mrs. Lehntman says it is a 'good house' (48). She assures Anna that 'it will be a good place' (49). But Anna knows better: 'She could not believe that it was best. No, it was very bad' (49). However, 'Anna gave all her savings for this place . . . for when Anna once began to make it nice, she could not leave it be until it was as good as for the purpose it should be' (50). After the house is fixed up, Mrs. Lehntman seems to lose interest in it. The narrator suggests that she is distracted, too distracted to take care of business. Still, the narrator insists that 'she was good and kind to all the people in her house, and let them do whatever they thought best' (50). The question remains: is it good to sacrifice yourself for others in exchange for the right to manage their lives (Anna's goodness), or is it good to be careless and to let one's children and associates do as they wish (Mrs. Lehntman's goodness).

And what of the 'good' purpose to which Mrs. Lehntman plans to put the house? In fact, Mrs. Lehntman becomes involved with an 'evil doctor', presumably an abortionist, and the home for unwed mothers becomes a kind of abortion clinic. Mrs. Lehntman is reported as having 'gone altogether bad' (59). Less than ten pages later, however, Mrs. Lehntman is back in Anna's life and the narrator tells us that Mrs. Lehntman 'was really a good

woman' (65). Similarly, we are told that Mrs. Drehten is
good at the same time that her abusive, alcoholic husband
is described as good. In other words, 'The Good Anna'
shows us that goodness is difficult, if not impossible to
define.

Furthermore, fixed definitions of good can be harm-
ful, as we see in 'The Gentle Lena'. Lena works in
the household of a Miss Aldrich, a household run by
'a cook who scolded Lena a great deal but . . . the good
incessant woman really only scolded so for Lena's good'
(217). Anna appears to have been transposed, nameless
but easily identifiable, from one story to the next. Having
read of Anna's own end, we are wary of the cook's notion
of 'Lena's good'. Indeed, the cook urges Lena to marry
the good Herman and to endure the conditions in the
household of the good Kreders. When Lena comes to the
cook in despair, she advises, 'You go home now and you
be good the way I tell you Lena' (248). However, this is
not good advice, for in the Kreder household, which does
not appear to be a good place for any sensitive person to
be, 'nobody ever noticed much what Lena wanted, and
she never really knew herself what she needed' (244). In
this environment Lena becomes 'dull, and lifeless' (252),
and finally dies.

The idea that meaning does not inhere in words themselves is explored most fully in 'Melanctha' because in
that story the characters join the reader in trying to understand the language they use. The reader's difficulty in
extracting stable meaning from words is intensified in
'Melanctha' by the disappearence of the narrative voice
and the narrative line for pages on end. In 'Melanctha'
the word 'good' that was so problematic in the earlier
stories appears again. It is first applied to Sam Johnson,
Rose's husband, a 'good man of the negroes' (78). At
this point in the story we hear very little about Sam
other than that he marries Rose, works regularly as a

deck hand on a coastal steamer and makes 'good wages' (80). Goodness is thus associated with financial stability and proper marriage.

'Good' is next used to describe John, a friend of Melanctha's father and 'a decent coloured coachman' at a stable 'near where Melanctha and her mother lived' (83–4). Like the good Sam's goodness, the good John's decency is associated with his 'prosperous house' (83) and his proper marriage. Melanctha is twelve years old when she knows John, and 'her good friend' John thinks 'about Melanctha . . . as if she were the eldest of his children' (84). However, the narrative strongly suggests that John takes a more than paternal interest in Melanctha. One night when John and Melanctha's father, James Herbert, are drinking together,

> The good John began to tell the father what a fine girl he had for a daughter. Perhaps the good John had been drinking a good deal of liquor, perhaps there was a gleam of something softer than the feeling of a friendly elder in the way John then spoke of Melanctha. There had been a good deal of drinking and John certainly that very morning had felt strongly Melanctha's power as a woman. James Herbert . . . looked very black and evil as he sat and listened while John grew more and more admiring as he talked . . . of the virtues and the sweetness of Melanctha. (85)

Suddenly the conversation erupts into a knife fight. The narrator comments laconically,

> John was a decent, pleasant, good natured, light brown Negro, but he knew how to use a razor to do bloody slashing.
> When the two men were pulled apart . . . John had not been much wounded but James Herbert had gotten

one good strong cut that went from his right shoulder
down across the front of his whole body. (85)

The implications of the word 'good' change through
association with drinking and bloody slashing, and our
evaluation of John changes too. He is still a good husband
and father and a good provider as he has always been, but
now we also know him as a good fighter, and we now
question whether he is a good friend for Melanctha. In
just this way does the word 'good' slip from its moorings
as it is applied to Jeff and to Melanctha. Jeff is introduced
as the good doctor. Certainly, he is a good son and a
good citizen, too, but as we have seen from Melanctha's
analysis of his character, he is not as good as he appears
to be. Later, however, Melanctha admits, 'Jeff you always
been very good always to me' (188); yet, in fact, he has
often been a bad lover and a bad friend to Melanctha.
Melanctha has a reputation as a bad woman, yet we see
that she is very good to her friends and that she is good to
Jeff until the end of the relationship when she is very bad
indeed. Jeff is usually torn between thinking Melanctha is
bad and believing she is good. Through his conversations
with her, Jeff has learned to question his definition of 'good'
and to allow for a definition that might embrace Melanctha.
Though Melanctha makes him suffer, 'he had learned [from
her] to have real love in him. That was very good to have
inside him' (189).

Having read about the good John and having been taken
through Jeff and Melanctha's lengthy considerations of
each other's goodness, we are then reintroduced to the
good Sam Johnson. As readers, we have been trained by
the process of reading this text to suspect the narrator's
unthinking labels and the narrator him/herself. Thus, when
we read that 'Rose was now to be married to a decent good
man of the Negroes' and that 'She [Rose] knew he [Sam]
was a good man and worked hard and got good wages'

(192–3), we are reminded of the good John and the good Jeff (and the good Anna before them), and we wonder how good Sam really is and in what sense he is good.

When Sam and Rose are first married, Melanctha is dating Jem Richards, and so she sees little of the newlyweds. At this time, so the narrator tells us, Sam does not like Melanctha, but he is good to her for Rose's sake. 'Rose was always telling Sam he must be good to poor Melanctha' (194). As Melanctha's relationship with Jem begins to break apart, she begins spending more and more time with Rose. This suits Rose because she is pregnant and lazy and enjoys being waited on by Melanctha. Sam is now good to Melanctha because she is good to Rose. 'Sam Johnson was always now very gentle and kind and good to Melanctha who had been so good to Rose in her bad trouble' (205). Gradually, however, Sam's goodness to Melanctha takes on a life and intensity of its own. 'Sam Johnson in these days was always very good and gentle to Melanctha. Sam was now beginning to be very sorry for her' (206). And then, 'Sam Johnson always, more and more, was good and gentle to Melanctha. Poor Melanctha, she was so good and sweet to do anything anybody ever wanted, and Melanctha always liked it if she could have peace and quiet, and always she could only find new ways to be in trouble. Sam often said this now to Rose about Melanctha' (208). And finally, 'Sam always was good and gentle to her [Melanctha], and Sam liked the ways Melanctha had to be quiet to him, and to always listen as if she was learning, when she was there and heard him talking, and then Sam liked the sweet way she always did everything so nicely for him' (209).

Although the narrator keeps insisting on Sam's goodness, the reader, remembering John's goodness, must see more in Sam's feeling for Melanctha than mere goodness. Apparently Rose too sees something objectionable in Sam's response to Melanctha, for, after having defended Melanctha's goodness to Sam (urging him to be good to her), she now tells Sam how bad Melanctha is. Sam, who does not like to argue, does not defend Melanctha as a good friend should. Rose begins to deny Melanctha access to Sam, sending her away before Sam comes home from work. She claims now to believe the bad things people say about Melanctha, and she finally tells Melanctha that she and Sam 'don't never any more want you to be setting your foot in my house' (213). The narrator never does explain this shift in Rose's feelings. Is Rose simply a bad friend? The narrator implies that this is so, at the same time insisting on Sam and Melanctha's goodness. But as readers we understand that Sam's goodness as a husband would not preclude his feeling attracted to Melanctha. This is what Rose understands as she listens to him talk about Melanctha; this is what we understand in Sam's words and in the narrator's repeated insistence on Sam's goodness. We also understand that 'good' tells us little about the meaning of goodness, and that 'good' as a descriptive label gives us very little understanding of the person to whom it is applied. Understanding comes only from listening to each utterance and experiencing each narrative moment; understanding is an ongoing process, always fluid, never fixed.

We can appreciate this fluidity most keenly when we cover the same narrative gound repeatedly, as 'Melanctha' forces us to do. If meaning were fixed, then repetition would reveal nothing new. But as Stein's narrative repetitions show, each pass over the same ground adds new information and alters our perception of the situation. As the narrator says of Melanctha's experience,

> It was still the same . . . only now for Melanctha somehow it was different, for though it was always the same thing that happened it had a different flavour . . . and dimly she began to see what it was that she should understand. (94–5)

Here (and throughout 'Melanctha') Stein uses time mark-
ers ('still', 'always' and 'now') to suggest that something
can be repeated over time yet be different in each present
instant of its occurrence.

Let us consider how this principle works in the narrative.
The narrative line in 'Melanctha' is always a circle; the
plot and subplots double back on themselves, and we hear
of many events and conversations at least twice: once at
the beginning of the narrative line, before we can truly
understand them, and once again at the end after we have
been through the process of the story coming into being.
For example, in the narrative of the good coachman John,
we are first briefly introduced to John as a good family man.
We already know something of Melanctha as a child (that
she is difficult to manage) and of her parents (her mother
is sweet and ineffectual; her father is coarse and brutal).
We know that Melanctha hates but respects her father
and does not like her mother very well. We are told
that Melanctha's father knows John; then, we are given
a report of a confrontation between Melanctha's parents
that transpired 'one day':

> One day James Herbert came to where his wife and
> daughter lived, and he was furious.
> 'Where's that Melanctha girl of yours,' he said fiercely,
> 'if she is to the Bishops' stables again, with that man John,
> I swear I kill her. Why don't you see to that girl better
> you, you're her mother.' (83)

At this time, such a fierce threat seems unwarranted, and
James Herbert's words seem proof of the correctness of the
narrator's view of him as unpleasant, unendurable, coarse,
angry, brutal and rough. This reported conversation is
followed by the story of John's friendship with Melanctha
and of the fight between John and James Herbert. After the
fight, when James Herbert has been 'put to bed to sleep

off his drinking and fighting', the narrative takes us to the
next day:

> The next day he [James Herbert] came to where his
> wife and daughter lived and he was furious.
> 'Where's that Melanctha, of yours?' he said to his wife,
> when he saw her. 'If she is to the Bishops' stables now
> with that yellow John, I swear I kill her. A nice way she
> is going for a decent daughter. Why don't you see to
> that girl better you, ain't you her mother!' (86)

We now realize that the earlier visit of James Herbert to
his wife, which precedes the story of the fight in narrative
time, actually follows it chronologically. The second time
we read James Herbert's words, we read them with a new
understanding based on our experience of the events that
brought those words into being. As we hear the words a
second time, we hear them differently than we did the first
time. In the second telling, James Herbert does not link
'girl' with his daughter's name, as he did earlier. Indeed,
her experience with John was the beginning of Melanctha's
feeling of her power as a woman. We realize now that James
Herbert is perhaps right to be concerned about Melanctha,
and we hear him say, as he did not say before (or as we did
not hear), 'A nice way she is going for a decent daughter'. In
fact, Melanctha is 'going' away from decency and into a life
of wandering in search of sexual experience. Knowledge of
the direction Melanctha's life is taking is what has enraged
James Herbert, but we understand the meaning behind his
words only on hearing them repeated – the same words, yet
different.

Another technique Stein uses to take us over the same
narrative ground in search of difference is to give us a
capsule narration from which the prose then pulls away,
like so much taffy, stretching and stretching the condensed
narration into an elongated process. For instance, the story

of Jeff and Melanctha is actually told in one paragraph preceding the longer telling of it that takes up most of 'Melanctha':

It was almost a year that she wandered [after Jane Harden] and then she met with a young mulatto. He was a doctor who had just begun to practise. He would most likely do well in the future, but it was not this that concerned Melanctha. She found him good and strong and gentle and very intellectual, and all her life Melanctha liked and wanted good and considerate people, and then too he did not at first believe in Melanctha. He held off and did not know what it was that Melanctha wanted. Melanctha came to want him very badly. They began to know each other better. Things began to be very strong between them. Melanctha wanted him so badly that now she never wandered. She just gave herself to this experience. (98–9)

This paragraph does not tell the complete story. Most obviously it does not take us to the end of the story (though we have no way of knowing this as we read it). But more subtly, the statement 'she found him good' hardly touches the tortuous process through which Melanctha comes to find this, nor does it convey how tenuous the finding is. The phrase, 'all her life Melanctha liked and wanted good and considerate people', is so often repeated in connection with Melanctha as to be a sort of refrain. By the time we read it here, we have already read it several times, most recently in the story of the good John. There it read: 'Melanctha always loved and wanted peace and gentleness and goodness and all her life for herself poor Melanctha could only find new ways to be in trouble' (85). In its later appearance, it is the same yet different; the end ('Melanctha could only find new ways to be in trouble') has been lopped off. As it stands, the paragraph outlining this new relationship of Melanctha with the young mulatto doctor suggests a happy outcome; however, the truncated refrain buried in the paragraph predicts a less happy end, but only to those who listen well or read carefully. The process which stretches before the reader at the end of this paragraph will, of course, bear out that subtle prediction. Therefore, the reader of 'Melanctha' must pay special attention not to what she is told by the narrator or the characters, but to the process of the telling, to what can be heard if a reader will enter the experience of the telling.

This emphasis on process did not come from Stein's study of the model of narrative prose urged on her by Leo.[10] It came from her study of two painters, Cézanne and Picasso.[11] In the winter before she began *Three Lives*, she and Leo had purchased Cézanne's *Portrait of Madame Cézanne with a Fan*. They had trouble deciding between this portrait and one of a man.

> [Ambroise] Vollard [the art dealer] said of course ordinarily a portrait of a woman always is more expensive than a portrait of a man but, said he looking at the picture very carefully, I suppppose with Cézanne it does not make any difference. They [Gertrude and Leo] put it in a cab and they went home with it. It was this picture that Alfy Maurer used to explain was finished and that you could tell that it was finished because it had a frame.
>
> It was an important purchase because in looking and looking at this picture Gertrude Stein wrote Three Lives.
>
> She had begun not long before as an exercise in literature to translate Flaubert's Trois Contes and then she had this Cézanne and she looked at it and under its stimulus she wrote Three Lives. (ABT 33–4)

In what way had this portrait stimulated her? She reveals the answer indirectly in her telling of the story of its purchase. It does not make any difference whether the Cézanne portrait is of a man or of a woman because in a Cézanne portait neither the person represented nor the exactness of the representation is as important as the process of making the painting. Madame Cézanne has a mask-like face; from behind the chalky mask, her dark eyes peer anonymously. We do not understand her from studying this image of her. What we do understand is how this painting was constructed. The painting is flat (no chiaroscuro, no perspective); it calls attention to its surface, to the technique of the brush strokes. That technique in turn calls attention to the process of seeing – the way in which an image is created out of our multiple perceptions of an object. In that sense, one can say that the painting is never 'finished' since it models two ongoing processes – seeing and painting – only arbitrarily completed, as it were, by the framing.

Picasso too was influenced by Cézanne, and his portrait of Stein shows that influence quite clearly. Like Madame Cézanne, Stein is posed at a three-quarter angle; her hands rest, as Madame Cézanne's do, on her lap; the armchair curves behind her head, the line of its curve separating the figure from the ground; Stein's face, too, is a mask, her eyes dark and blank. Yet the similarities between the images are less important than the similarity in the execution, the emphasis both painters placed on the coming into being of the image through the performance of the artist as seer and creator.[12] And this similarity could hardly have escaped Stein, sitting for her portrait as she did every day and every night across from the portrait of Madame Cézanne. At Picasso's studio Stein saw that daily for ninety days, Picasso stared at the same object (herself) and painted again and again the same image (her portrait). Yet, every day this image changed. Her vision of her portrait would have been like a palimpsest, her mind's eye retaining previous images that Picasso had erased. Gertrude Stein witnessed Picasso's portrait of her recording the process of its own creation. Its meaning for both artist and model was in this process, not in the final image or in its resemblance to or representation of the model. This was a lesson Stein was to take to heart (unlike the 'exercise in literature'). It changed the way she wrote. We can see this change beginning in *Three Lives*, with its increasing emphasis on the process of making and communicating meaning.

3 Beyond Narrative: *The Making of Americans*

In 1906, having completed *Three Lives*, Gertrude Stein took up once again the unfinished novel, *The Making of Americans*, which she had begun in 1903. According to Leon Katz, who has worked extensively with Stein's early manuscripts and notebooks, Stein began in 1906 making notes toward revising the old material.[1] It is not known how many chapters she had originally written since she destroyed part of the early manuscript, but she preserved its first five chapters, and these were to serve as the starting point of the new version of *The Making of Americans*, a novel which was eventually to run to 925 pages and to take five years to write. When we compare the extant text of the original to the revised version which occupies the first thirty-four pages of the completed novel, we can see exactly how drastically Stein's purposes and procedures had changed from 1903 to 1906. Furthermore, if we compare the first thirty-four pages, in which Stein balanced the old way of writing and the new, to the rest of *The Making of Americans*, most of it written between 1908 and 1911, we can see an even more radical change taking place in Stein's style and in her approach to the business of writing.

In the original version of the novel, Stein is clearly imitating the models of English narrative she had studied in the reading room of the British Museum. Austen and Trollope come to mind. The original *Making of Americans* is a domestic novel about the marriage of the eldest daughter of the Dehning family. (Stein had begun to tell of the marriage of the second daughter,

but the part of the mansucript in which she would
have developed this second story was destroyed.) In
this earlier work, Stein is interested in the psychology of her characters and the sociological implications
of their behaviour. The bemused narrator, who, Katz
suggests, is modelled on the narrators in John Lyly's
Euphues, which Stein was reading at the time,[2] seems
to approve and admire the solid, middle-class virtues
represented by the Dehnings while declaring himself
to be a 'Brother Singular', misplaced in his generation
and disapproved by his fellow citizens. Nonetheless,
this singular fellow seems secure in the belief that the
reader will share his point of view, which turns out to
be the fairly conventional one that young daughters of
the bourgeoisie should not marry romantic adventurers
who promise exciting lives but should marry their own
kind. Despite the narrator's protestations that what he
means to write 'is not a simple novel with a plot
and conversations' (FQED 144) and despite his suggestion that what he writes may not please us, the
narrative style is as traditional as the moral of the
story. Characters and scenes are conventionally described
and conversations conventionally recorded. The narrative structure is orderly, the narration concise. Each
of the five chapters is carefully focused on a single
narrative goal: We are first introduced to the Dehning
parents, then to the children, focusing on Julia, the
eldest daughter and the heroine of this part of the
novel; we then hear of the meeting and romance between
Julia and Henry Hersland and of the Dehning's initial disapproval but eventual acceptance of the match,
culminating in the wedding of the two; we end with
the foreshadowing of the unhappy consequences of the
marriage.

Stein retains all of this material in the revised version.
She also reproduces verbatim passages from the old

manuscript. For example, the realistic descriptions of the Dehning country and city houses, first written in 1903, reappear in 1906 with only a few, insignificant, one-word alterations (see FQED 138–9 and 161; and MOA 12 and 28). The same is true of the descriptions of Mr. and Mrs. Dehning and of their conversations with each other and with their children. These remnants of the old manuscript are arresting in their new context because they are so remarkably different from the writing that surrounds them.

As might be expected, the new writing has some of the characteristics of *Three Lives*. For instance, when the narrator introduces the grandfather of Julia Dehning, he describes him as a 'decent well-meaning faithful good-enough ordinary man' (MOA 6), an adjective string like those in *Three Lives*. When grandfather Dehning speaks, he sounds like the German immigrants in 'The Gentle Lena' and 'The Good Anna'. Henry Dehning, his son and Julia's father, has also acquired immigrant speech which he did not have in the original manuscript. Early in the new novel, in paragraphs that Stein has added to the old manuscript, we find many occurrences of the words 'good' and 'always', again reminiscent of *Three Lives*. The narrator's comments about Henry Dehning sound like earlier characterizations of Jeff Campbell: 'A man like Dehning never can feel it real to himself, things as they were in his early manhood, now that he has made his life and habits and his feelings all so different . . . it can never anymore be really present to his feeling' (MOA 7). But the echoes of *Three Lives* do not persist. The changes Stein makes from one version of *The Making of Americans* to the next do not show her allegiance to the form and style discovered in *Three Lives* so much as they show her interest in narrative and linguistic territories as yet unknown and unexplored.

As Stein copies parts of the old manuscript, she keeps her mind open to new possibilities, and copying leads to creation, but creation of a very different sort than one would normally expect in a revision. She does not seek to adapt or expand the old; rather, she seeks to move away from it. Creation of the new comes through digression from the old. For instance, in the old manuscript, Julia's brother George, is introduced as follows:

> The boy George named under the Anglo Saxon influence bid fair to do credit to his christening. He was a fair athletic chap, cheery as his father, full of excellent intentions and elaborated purposes and though these generally were lost on their way to fulfillment you must remember he was at this time scarcely fourteen that period which has been so well called in boys the senseless age, and so do not make too much of any present weakness.
>
> For us as well as for Mrs. Dehning the important matter in the family history at this moment is the marriage of Julia the eldest daughter. (FQED 145–6)

Thus, the narrator draws us back into the narrative, focusing our attention on the center, Julia, after only the briefest side trip for a quick character sketch of a younger family member.

In the new novel, George makes his appearance as follows:

> After Julia came the boy George and he was not named after his grandfather. And so it was right that in his name he should not sound as if he were the son of his father, so at least his mother decided for him, and the father, he laughed and let her do the way she liked it. And so the boy was named George and the other was there but hidden as an initial to be only used for signing.
>
> The boy George bade fair to do credit to his christening. George Dehning now about fourteen was strong in sport

and washing. He was not foreign in his washing. Oh, no, he was really an american.

It's a great question this question of washing.

(MOA 15)

With this, the narrator is off and running with a long and amusing digression on washing. Unlike the short characterization of George in the earlier manuscript, this digression is not curtailed in the interests of maintaining our focus on 'the important matter' in the history. In fact, the attention given to the digression suggests that there is no hierarchy of importance in this new narrative. Furthermore, the digression serves no apparent narrative purpose. We hear about washing because of some associative process of the narrator which we can only dimly guess at. Perhaps he was reminded of washing because the name of the character suggested another George – George Washing[ton]. Or perhaps he associated cleanliness with the German-American middle class to which George Dehning belongs. In either case, we are no longer following the story; rather, we are following the thought process of the narrator. This activity, normally relegated to the background of a narrative (and most often repressed entirely), is foregrounded, called to our attention, and the narrative is thereby reformed. Associative digression becomes the new structuring principle of *The Making of Americans*.

In a sense, almost all of the book is a digression from the story introduced in its first thirty pages. Although Julia Dehning and Alfred Hersland (Stein changes his first name) get married on page 33, Stein writes on page 607, 'Alfred Hersland and Jula Dehning came to have some loving feeling and then they came to marrying. I am beginning again a history of them'. On page 637, she writes

I am going now again to commence my regular description of being in Julia Dehning, of Dehning family living,

of Julia's meeting and marrying and loving and not
learning, and not enduring Alfred Hersland, and of
her complete living. I am beginning again, not from
the beginning this time that is certain.

And two pages later:

Julia Dehning and Alfred Hersland came to be married
ones, I am describing this thing. (MOA 639)

The 574 pages intervening between page 33 and page 607
have been a monumental digression from the original
subject of the narrative.

Stein digresses in order to tell the story of another family,
the Herslands of Gossols, the family that produced Alfred
Hersland who comes east and marries Julia Dehning. (The
Herslands are based loosely on Stein's immediate family,
Gossols being a thinly disguised Oakland, California).[3]
Within this major digression are many minor digressions,
since each time Stein introduces a new character, she
seems to feel compelled to give the history of that person
(including a history of his or her family). This is true of
important characters – David Hersland (Alfred's father)
and his wife Fanny Hissen Hersland, for instance – and
of unimportant characters as well – the family dressmaker,
for example.

The frequent digressions require that the story of the
Herslands begin again and again. (A common refrain in
the novel is 'as I was saying'.) Each time we return to
the original point of departure, we have made a circle (the
structure of 'Melanctha'). Rather than closing the circle and
moving on, however, we often return over the same path
and trace the same circle. Therefore, the digressions entail
a tremendous amount of repetition, both on a macrocosmic
and a microcosmic level: Events are repeated, but so are
words, phrases, sentences and strings of sentences. This
digressing and repeating stretches the narrative over an

enormous space. Everything takes longer to tell, and paragraphs and sentences expand to accommodate the telling.

As the structure of the narrative expands, so does its purpose. To begin with Stein planned to give us the history of a single family's progress, confident that this particular history could be representative of the making of Americans – all Americans. Thus, in the earlier manuscript, we hear that 'Julia Dehning at eighteen was a very vigorous specimen of self-satisfied domineering American girlhood' (FQED 146); that 'Mrs. Dehning was the quintessence of loud voiced good-looking prosperity' (FQED 140); and that 'strong friendships outside the members of the house are never the tradition of such a bourgeois family life. Julia had no such friends' (FQED 170). The narrator presents the characters as specimens and is comfortable with the reasoning process whereby these specimens give rise to conclusions about their race, class, gender, ethnicity and age. One can say that this is a nineteenth-century view of human nature, and it matches an equally nineteenth-century view of history articulated in the first paragraph of the old manuscript:

> It has always seemed to me a rare privilege this of being an American, a real American and yet one whose tradition it has taken scarcely sixty years to create. We need only realise our parents, remember our grandparents and know ourselves and our history is complete. The old people in a new world, the new people made out of the old that is the story that I mean to tell for that is what really is and what I really know. (FQED 137)

As Stein digresses from the original manuscript, she completely overturns the view that human nature can ever be generalized from particular specimens and the view that history is a linear progression toward eventual completion. Stein comes to espouse the belief that each person is unique;

therefore, Stein's history must be 'a history of everyone who ever were or are or will be living' (MOA 294) – a history that may never finish, a history in which each moment is infinitely expandable.

This new history is arrived at by experiencing each moment's plenitude. Stein thinks of a whole and then atomizes it, parts proliferating with greater and greater acceleration until recording them seems almost beyond the power of the writer. If the whole is a person, David Hersland, for example, Stein records the minute gradations of character in that person. If the whole is a category, for example, men who 'have it in them to be as big as all the world in their beginning, they are strong in their beginning' (MOA 117), she thinks of everyone she knows who fits into the category and the exact degree to which they exhibit the attribute identified in the category. But she seldom names these members of the category, referring to them instead by indefinite pronouns – one, many, some, each. In this way she gives the illusion of covering all of humanity. She thus gives a history of the whole by ostensibly recording all of its smallest parts.

Her goal in this minute cataloguing is to describe the 'bottom nature' of each person in her history of everyone, his or her defining characteristic. At the same time, she tries to find the 'resemblances' among 'kinds' of men and women. Both goals can be accomplished by the writer sensitive to repetition. Stein tells us:

> Always then I listen and come back again and again to listen to every one. Always then I am thinking and feeling the repeating in every one. Sometimes it happens that I have a complete history of some one, of the meaning of all the repeating in them the first time I look hard at them, mostly this is in me a slow thing, learning understanding, mostly I come back again and again to listen to the repeating in every one before they are

a whole one, before there is to me a whole history of the being in them. Always I come back again and again, it has happened that sometimes I have had the whole history of some one the first time I looked long at them, mostly this is a slow thing, always even when understanding happens like with this one the first time of hard looking, always, then I go back again and again to listen, to fill in, to be certain. (MOA 316)

By listening to the ways people repeat themselves, one can 'realize' their bottom natures, see the whole history of any one of them. In a similar fashion, by being aware of the ways in which one person repeats another. one can begin to see resemblances. These resemblances allow for the creation of a system: the history we are reading.

> Everybody then is mostly a real one to me, everybody is now like some one and like some other one and then again like some other one and each one sometimes is a whole one to me.
>
> This being resembling, this seeing resemblances between those one is knowing is interesting, defining, confusing, uncertain and certain. . . . This is then a beginning of learning to make kinds of men and women. Slowly then all the resemblances between one and all the others that have something, different things in common with that one, all these fall into an ordered system sometime then that one is a whole one . . . all resemblances in that one must be counted in, nothing must ever be thrown out, everything in each one must be included to know that one. (MOA 340)

Repetition can reveal life patterns at the same time that it records differences.

As the preceding passages show, Stein is describing for us her process of composition. This process involves two activities: knowing and telling. 'Sometime, then I know it,

sometime then I tell it. There are many ways of knowing,
as I have been telling, there are many ways of telling' (MOA
325). In the old manuscript Stein announced her narrator's
intention to tell 'a story', confident that the story is what
really is and what is really known (FQED 137). In the new
version, she continues to try to tell the story of a family's
progress, but she is trying at the same time to tell another
story, the story of her own cognitive processes. In telling
the story of her own knowing and telling, Stein has no need
for a narrator, for who is better suited to tell this story than
Gertrude Stein herself.

The disappearance of the non-authorial narrator is perhaps the most significant change from the early manuscript
version of *The Making of Americans* and from *Three Lives*
to the new version of *The Making of Americans*. Both the
early manuscript and *Three Lives* have narrators who are
distinct from the author. In the early manuscript, Stein
follows the narrative convention of using a narrator who
tells the tale and who thus seems to be the one who has
written down the events of the story. The text is simply
a transparent window onto the tale, a story which already
exists (it really is) and has only to be known. In a sense,
this narrator is a reader of events, and in this sense he is our
'brother', as his frequent addresses to us and his use of the
inclusive 'we' suggest. From his tone, we can almost picture
him next to us, his arm around our shoulders, as together
we gaze at the scene and note the particulars of the 'lives'
the 'history' of which we are about 'to hear' (FQED 144).
In *Three Lives*, the narrator is not a stand-in for the writer
or an ally of the reader; rather, he is another character in
the story, a sort of informant (the neighbourhood gossip,
perhaps) of limited insight and intelligence. Although Stein
increasingly blurs the distinction between the voices of the
narrator and the characters in *Three Lives*, she maintains
the distinction between the narrator and herself, as the
writer. The writer's activity of constructing the narrative

to make and communicate meaning is thus separate from the narrator's telling. In *Three Lives* 'what really is' is not a story visible through the window of the text; 'what really is' is, in fact, the text itself, opaque with patterning, the site of knowledge. We must 'read' it in order to understand the story told by the narrator.

In the new *Making of Americans*, we have no need of a narrator since the story of the Dehnings and Herslands is not presented as anterior to the story of the making of the text. Their story evolves from the writer's attempts to know that story and to tell it; the family's progress and the writer's process are told as though they are synchronous, and *The Making of Americans* becomes a history of both at the same time. As Stein prepares to leave the early manuscript and move forward into the new novel, she reproduces and adapts an address to the reader from the early manuscript. A comparison of the two shows how the relationship between text and story has changed.

From the old manuscript:

> Bear it in mind my reader if indeed there be any such that the thing I mean to write here is not a simple novel with a plot and conversations but a record of a family progress respectably lived and to be carefully set down and so arm yourself with patience for you must hear more of the character of these four children before we can proceed with the story of their lives as they one after the other grow old enough to determine their own fortune and their own relations. (FQED 144)

From the revision:

> Bear it in your mind my reader, but truly I never feel it that there ever can be for me any such a creature, no it is this scribbled and dirty and lined paper that is really to be to me always my receiver, – but anyhow reader, 5 bear it in your mind – will there be for me ever any

such a creature, – what I have said always before to
you, that this that I write down a little each day here
on my scraps of paper for you is not just an ordinary
kind of novel with a plot and conversations to amuse
10 you, but a record of a decent family progress respectably
lived by us and our fathers and our mothers, and our
grand-fathers, and grand-mothers, and this is by me
carefully a little each day to be written down here; and
so my reader arm yourself in every kind of a way to be
15 patient, and to be eager, for you must always have it
now before you to hear much more of these many kinds
of decent ordinary people, of old, grown, grand-fathers
and grand-mothers, of growing old fathers and growing
old mothers, of ourselves who are always to be young
20 grown men and women for us, and then there are still to
be others and we must wait and see the younger fathers
and young mothers bear them for us, these younger
fathers and young mothers who always are ourselves
inside us, who are to be always young grown men and
25 women to us. And so listen while I tell you all about
us, and wait while I hasten slowly forwards, and love,
please, this history of this decent family's progress.

(MOA 33–4)

In the revised passage, the site of the family's history is
not Bridgepoint or Gossols, but the very lined paper on
which that history is written. The writing, like the history
it tells, is an ongoing process that may never end (see ll.
7–8 and 12–16). In the first passage there is a 'before'
and an 'after'. The generations move in linear sequence.
'Fortunes' and 'relations' are 'determined', suggesting an
end to the progress. The history told in the second passage,
on the other hand, begins with 'us' and works its way from
the present to the past generations and then forward again
(see ll. 10–12 and 17–20). There is no longer a clear,
linear progression of generations as there was in the

earlier passage. In the first passage, pronoun reference is unambiguous, and therefore the narrative point of view is clear. There is an 'I', the narrator telling the story, and a 'you', the reader; both make a 'we', who together watch 'them' (the other), those family members whose orderly and finite progress the story records. In the second passage, the pronouns are confusing. The demonstrative pronoun 'this' in line 12 ('this is by me carefully, a little each day to be written down') could refer either to the progress of the family or to the record of that progress. The family progress and its record (the book being written, the book we are reading) are conflated by the ambiguous demonstrative pronouns. Personal pronouns have a similar effect throughout the passage. 'Them' on line 22 refers to fathers and mothers; however, the normal boundary between self and others imposed by the third person pronoun is not so clear as it was in the first passage. The second passage tells us that the fathers and mothers exist inside 'us'; 'they' are 'us' (ll. 22–24). This 'us' does not clearly refer to the writer and reader as it did in the first passage. It *could* have that meaning, but the writer has already denied the existence of a reader (ll. 1–2). Instead, 'us' seems to refer to the writer and the paper, the receiver of the writing (ll. 4, 20, and 22). 'Us' seems also to refer to the as yet unidentified offspring and descendants of the mothers and fathers (ll. 11 and 19). Both writer and receiver seem to have been generated by the mothers and fathers. However, the mothers and fathers exist inside 'us' (writer and receiver); in that case, the writing, the emptying every day of the writer's words onto the paper, generates this family. In other words, the family both gives birth to and originates in the act of writing.

A novel so conceived is a closed system. Such a novel, Stein's new version of *The Making of Americans*, is often about the process of its own construction, then, since that is a valid entrée into the story of the family's progress. The writer plans the writing as she writes:

But all this history of her [Fanny Hissen] will come later.
Now David Hersland is to be married to her and she is
to leave her family feeling all behind her.

Later there will be more talking of the natural Hissen
way of living. Later when the Hersland children have
grown to be ready to begin their later living then we will
know more of some of them. (67)

The writer despairs and instructs herself in ways to over-
come despair:

Sometime as I was saying there are so many ways of
seeing, feeling resemblances in some one, some one
resembles so many men and women that it is confusing,
baffling, then the one learning kinds in men and women
is despairing, nothing then to that one has any meaning,
it is then to that one all of it only an arbitrary choosing
and then that one must stop looking, that one then must
begin again then and always never forgetting anything
that one ever has seen as a resemblance in the one that
one is then learning. (341)

The writer succumbs to despair:

Perhaps no one ever will know the complete history of
every one. This is a sad thing. Perhaps no one will ever
have as a complete thing the history of any one. This is a
very sad thing. . . . Perhaps no one ever gets a complete
history of any one. This is very discouraging thinking. I
am very sad now in this feeling. (454)

The writer rejoices in her power:

There are many that I know then. They are all of them
repeating and I hear it, see it, feel it. More and more I
understand it. I love it, I tell it. I love it, I live it and I tell it.

> Always I will tell it. They live it and I see it and I hear it and I feel it. They live it and I see it and I hear it and I feel it and I love it, sometime then I understand it, sometime then there is a completed history of each one by it. (305)

Even when the writing is about the family, it is ultimately self-referential. For example, Stein is continually offering us 'descriptions' of family members, but these descriptions begin with a concept in the writer's mind (e.g. resisting, attacking, angry feeling, sensitiveness), and the description is an insistence on the existence of the quality. For example, the discussion of 'angry feeling' goes on for twenty-three pages. What follows is an excerpt, but not unlike the rest of the discussion:

> Angry feeling is certainly coming to be in them in some. It is really a surprising thing to some that they have been having really angry feeling in them. Some are certainly not feeling in them before, during, after they have been having angry feeling any of the feeling that would be for them in their thinking, in their feeling, in their realisation angry feeling. It is a curious thing that certainly certainly very many are not feeling any feeling in them giving to them angry feeling and yet certainly they are just then having angry feeling in them. This is happening quite often to some. Some are ones of such a kind of them and of some of such of them not many are knowing that they are having angry feeling in them when they are having angry feeling in them. In a way David Hersland quite often was of such of them. (774–5)

Stein does finally attach the concept to a named person, but that person exists in relation to the concept, and the concept exists only in the mind of Gertrude Stein. This is description as tautology. The proliferation of indefinite pronouns adds to this effect since indefinite pronouns have no obvious reference point outside the mind of the person who originates them. They are like riddles (someone's sleeping in my bed), but in *The Making of Americans* the riddles of the indefinite pronouns are never solved.

Like her descriptions, the history Stein writes is predictably circular. In part, this is because of the incessant repetition, but it is also because of the way she manipulates verb tenses so that we are always trapped as readers in an eternal present. Events are always happening:

> I am remembering pretty completely everything I have been telling. I am always thinking I am not remembering what I am going to be telling what I have been telling but really I am remembering pretty well what I have been telling, what I am telling, what I am going to be telling. Now I am telling about some ways of having sensitiveness and learning in some having attacking being, independent dependent being in them.
>
> Julia Dehning as I have been saying was always resisting changing the attacking way she had had, was having, would be having all her living. As I was saying she had not really then sense for living. As I was saying she was not really an unsuccessful one in living. (634)

In this passage, past, present and future merge in a continuing present tense. One period of time is not clearly marked off from the next. We never look at an activity as completed; rather, we see that in its past it was present and in its future it will be present. It is always present because the telling is always present to Stein as she writes and to us as we read. Even in the last two sentences with clear past tense verbs, the participial 'as I was saying' makes clear that the action referred to is not a past action so much as it is a past telling in this presently unfolding story. As Stein was saying something about this action, it was happening. In *The Making of Americans*, every action is present as it is told, and every telling refers to another telling. The frequent use of the present participle creates a prose in which everything seems to be going on at the same time. Progress is process.

Stein's syntax intensifies the effects of immediacy and circularity produced by her content, her narrative structure and her use of indefinite pronouns and participial verbs. We can best understand how this syntax works by considering a sentence which is typical of many such in *The Making of Americans*. This is a sentence long enough to be its own paragraph:

> I see so many who I am very certain will not be at all interested in my being certain that each one is himself inside him, that each one is of a kind in men and women, that I can make a diagram now including a
> 5 very considerable number of kinds in men and women and that sometime I will be able to explain the being in each one and make a scheme of relations in kinds of being with each one having in them the way of eating, thinking, feeling, working, drinking, loving, beginning
> 10 and ending, feeling things as being existing of their kind of being, with sensitivenesses and suddenesses and impatient and patient and dependent and independent being of their kind of them and succeeding and failing of their kind of them and I will be able to make groups
> 15 of them and it will be such an interesting and such an important thing in my feeling, in my being, and I will be making groups of them of each kind of them with some of each kind of them succeeding some failing some in between succeeding and failing, some having more of
> 20 something of their kind of them in them than other things of their kind of them and each one then I am ever knowing comes sometime then to be such a clear one to my feeling and I could want to have every one know every one so that each one could see the meaning of my
> 25 explanation and always I am certain that so very many I

am always knowing are not wanting to completely listen
to me in my explaining and many are not understanding
that they must be hearing me completely and they are
not doing this thing and here I am and I am certain,
30 at least I am mostly always certain and yet always I
am of the dependent independent kind of them and
always in me there is quite a good deal always of
dependent despairing and always I am knowing and
always I will be knowing always now I am certain that
35 mostly those I am knowing do not want, cannot be
completely listening and it is such a complete being in
me and I am important that is certain and here I am
full up now with knowing that mostly those to whom
I am explaining are not completely hearing. (595)

This sentence, a series of restrictive and parallel clauses,
creates a dense and immobile fabric of words that stops
even the most energetic reader at its surface. At first glance
it seems unreadable; at second glance, indecipherable. Yet,
of course, it can be read and it has meaning. It begins
with the writer's simple assertion that she sees many (here
'sees' means 'knows' or 'knows of'). All subsequent bits
of information depend for their existence on that original
sighting, and the original sighting has no meaning (is
incomplete) without the subsequent bits of information.
The 'many' Stein sees are people 'who . . . will not be at
all interested in [her] being certain' about a number of
things. Lines 1–25 tell what those things are in a series of
restrictive dependent clauses that seem to go on indefinitely,
forcing us to wait interminably for closure, the completion
of meaning. The coordinate conjunctions between clauses,
which are supposed to match and join sentence parts,
actually produce a kind of disjunction since they create a
catalogue or list, a form which suggests that one element
is as important as the next, that no part of the sentence has
preeminence over another. In other words, this sentence

is more paratactic than hypotactic despite the presence of coordinate conjunctions; the clauses are placed one after another without any indication of the relations among them other than spatial contiguity and mutual dependence on the original clause. Without subordination, the sentence is a uniform mass of language, and we must get through all of it if we are to understand any of it.

One of the things about which Stein is certain is what she 'sees' to begin with, that is, 'many who will not be at all interested in [her] being certain'. If she is certain about this original observation, as her parenthetic 'I am certain' on line 1 tells us, then it follows that many are not interested in this 'seeing' that is to be reported; thus, the sentence has a circular and self-cancelling effect. Its circularity opposes the linearity and forward movement of syntax; its self-cancellation seems to erase the meaning as it is made. Within a sentence like this, time stops; we go nowhere because the sentence goes nowhere. Although it goes on and on, filling the page, it makes no progress. It is what Stein would call a 'continuous present'.

If we push ahead (or are pulled ahead by the march of words across the page), we reach the series of parallel independent clauses beginning in line 25 with 'and always I am certain', parallel to the first clause, 'I see so many'. These parallel independent clauses add new items to the list of things about which Stein is certain; all are variations of the initial worry about her readers: As her readers will not be interested, so they will not want to listen completely, will not understand and will not hear completely. The restrictive clauses describe what she is certain that she is doing in writing *The Making of Americans* (making a diagram, making a scheme of relations, making groups), and the parallel independent clauses describe the reader response she imagines. The entire sentence, then, is focused on the process of making and communicating meaning. This is not to say that it is completely self-referential since it also refers to the 'people' (those who eat, think, feel, work, drink, love and so forth) whose history Stein is writing. Nonetheless, the sentence tells us far less about them than it does about Stein's interest in the processes of writing and reading, our mutual endeavors.

If we want to listen to and to hear Stein completely, then we must enter her process of knowing and explaining. She challenges us to become active readers, for such a sentence explicitly demands such a reader in order to be understood. Sentences like this assert their presence; by their very length they suggest the substantiality of language. They are bulky, inescapably there, occupying space.

Stein ends the sentence by declaring that she is full up with what she knows (with her sentence). She is a constantly replenished reservoir of knowledge and language; even as she empties herself onto the page, she is filling with new knowledge, ready to spill forth in the next sentence. Stein's inexhaustibility is evident in the length and density of *The Making of Americans*. Even when one reaches the last of the 925 pages, one has no sense of completion. Gertrude Stein liked to remove paintings from their frames and to hang them unframed since she felt that the frames constrained the art. In *The Making of Americans*, she has removed the frame from narrative and allowed language to spill unconstrained into the pages of her notebooks. Even bound as it is between the covers of a single volume, *The Making of Americans* seems to resist enclosure. Because the writing is not finished or finishable, we need not attempt to read *The Making of Americans* from start to finish. We need only give our complete attention to each moment of reading (listening and hearing) for as long as we choose to read.

If composition is a process of discovery, as Stein believed it was, then the record of that process provides the reader with an analogous adventure in reading, a journey of discovery, perilous, but not without its pleasures and rewards. We need only be hardy travellers.

4 'Perfectly Unprecedented Arrangements': *Tender Buttons*

Written between 1911 and 1914 and divided into three sections – 'Objects', 'Food' and 'Rooms'[1] – *Tender Buttons* is a slim volume of prose poems, which Stein later called verbal 'still lifes'.[2] Other of Stein's works have received a greater quantity of critical attention (*Three Lives* and *The Autobiography of Alice B. Toklas* in particular), but none has provoked more imaginative – even fevered – interpretive activity than *Tender Buttons*. Because *Tender Buttons* is so full of interpretive clues, many readers, trained by years of symbol hunting, dutifully play detective, beginning with the question 'What is this about?', assembling the various clues into an interpretive system and arriving, finally, at the 'meaning' of the text.

In 1967, for example, Allegra Stewart argued that *Tender Buttons* was a 'mandala', a magic enclosure for the unconscious mind of the creator and thus a fit object for a Jungian analysis. In a 1978 article Pamela Hadas focused on the themes of loss, separation, change and restitution in the work and, giving them an autobiographical reading, concluded that *Tender Buttons* reflects Stein's pain at the loss of Leo and her hope that her relationship with Alice will be 'restitution' for that loss. In 1986 in an article with the provocative title, 'Woman as Eros-Rose in Gertrude

Stein's *Tender Buttons*', Doris Wright explained the poems as the encoding of lesbian sexuality. (This is a view held as well by Catharine Stimpson, Shari Benstock and, in part, by Neil Schmitz and William Gass.)[3] In her 1989 book on Stein's use of dialogue as a kind of feminist poetics, Harriet Chessman concluded that *Tender Buttons* 'expresses a yearning . . . for a loved female presence', though she added that this 'presence' 'goes beyond any one figure [Alice]' and is '"dreamed" about differently by different readers'.[4] Finally, in 1990, twenty-three years after Allegra Stewart's 'spiritual' reading of the poems, Lisa Ruddick finds in *Tender Buttons* a 'woman-centered, revisionary spirituality'. She interprets the text as representing 'Stein's fully developed vision of the making and unmaking of patriarchy'. Ruddick writes, 'An idea that she [Stein] develops here [in *Tender Buttons*] . . . is that patriarchy constitutes itself by a sacrifice, real or mythic. . . . What *Tender Buttons* then suggests is that once one sees male dominance as dependent on sacrifice, one is in a position to undo sacrifice and to transcend patriarchal thinking'.[5]

As imaginative as most of these interpretive systems are, however, *Tender Buttons* itself calls into question the very enterprise of interpretation, an irony which is not lost on the critics. Lisa Ruddick, for instance, qualifies her own readings: 'My readings are not meant to substitute for [the] experience of uncertainty and mobility [engendered by the text]'.[6] Ruddick writes, 'The witty, riddling structures of *Tender Buttons* amount to a lure as well as an obstacle [to interpretation]'.[7] That being so, some critics have concentrated, quite profitably, on the condition of indeterminacy created by a work that is at once 'lure' (with its suggestion of trickery by the author and danger for the reader) and 'obstacle' (with its suggestion of authorial resistance to the reader's interpretive activities). Marjorie Perloff advances the argument for indeterminacy most persuasively in *The Poetics of Indeterminacy*. She writes, 'The meaning [of

Tender Buttons] . . . remains latent, impossible to translate into something else'.[8]

If meaning is indeterminate, then discussions of what *Tender Buttons* is 'about' are likely to be unsatisfactory, especially when critics respond to the indeterminacy by offering readings which are overdetermined; rather than illuminating each other, such readings have the effect of cancelling each other out, and they are contrary to the spirit of the text. A more useful approach to this text (and to all of Stein's texts, in fact) is to ask not what it is about, but what it is doing. We can, as Marjorie Perloff suggests, look at *Tender Buttons* as a 'way of happening'.[9] This is the approach taken by Neil Schmitz, Jayne Walker and Marianne DeKoven, who all see *Tender Buttons* as a kind of authorial 'playing'. Schmitz writes that *Tender Buttons* 'records, moment by moment, the play of her [Stein's] mind with the world before her',[10] and in his book, *Of Huck and Alice*, he traces this 'record' brilliantly, showing 'how . . . we get' from the beginning to the end and revealing the humour in the play.[11] Jayne Walker calls language Stein's 'playground' and draws our attention to the seriousness of Stein's language play. She describes Stein as 'rigorously investigating its [language's] laws and testing its limits', an activity Walker finds analogous to cubist investigations of visual media and pictorial representation.[12] Marianne DeKoven sees *Tender Buttons* as anti-patriarchal, 'presymbolic *jouissance* and as irreducibly multiple, fragmented, open-ended articulation of lexical meaning'.[13] Whether we conclude that Stein's play is that of an American humorist (as Schmitz does), a cubist (Walker), or a feminist (DeKoven) will depend on our critical approach to this work. In other words, how a reader characterizes Stein's play will depend on who the reader is. The important matter is to recognize, as Schmitz, Walker and DeKoven do, that the 'meaning' of *Tender Buttons* is to be found not in its correspondence to an external reality (spiritual, autobiographical, socio-cultural), but in the operations of the text. We must ask ourselves what is happening in this text in order to understand it as a way of happening.

What is happening in *Tender Buttons* is what happens in every work by Gertrude Stein: She is writing; she is performing with language. In *Tender Buttons*, Stein uses language to invoke and inscribe the objects, actions, conditions and actors of her domestic environment. Thus, many of the interpretive clues in the work have led readers to conclude that *Tender Buttons* is autobiographical, and therefore, by extension, female or feminist, domestic and erotic. The world to which *Tender Buttons* refers is indeed a world where women sew, draw, play music, cook, eat and dress up. They wear petticoats and shirt waists; dresses, shoes and shawls; red hats and blue coats. Adorned with feathers, handkerchiefs, umbrellas and eyeglasses, they take tea and cake from new cups and saucers set out on steady tables; they have oranges and oatmeal for breakfast, lunch on roast beef and potatoes, and eat dinners of stews and soups cooked for them by other women. This was the world of Gertrude Stein and Alice Toklas. It is a world in which one woman loves another, rubs her till she purrs (475) and contemplates her 'shallow hole rose on red' (474). Although Stein is inscribing this world in her text through the nouns that name its objects, its places and its activities, she cannot be said to represent that world through her language. The objects which are named do not undergo a mimetic transformation from the object to discourse about the object or to discourse which anchors the name of the object in a linguistic matrix that seeks to reproduce the material context of the actual object. For example, the poem 'Rhubarb', reads:

Rhubarb is susan not susan not seat in *bunch* toys *not wild* and laughable not in little places *not in neglect* and

vegetable not in fold coal age not please. (489)
(emphasis added)

I have emphasised words in the poem that tell us something
about rhubarb – it is a cultivated vegetable ('not wild', does
not grow 'in neglect') which grows in 'bunches'. I must con-
fess, however, that I first got my information about rhubarb
from the encyclopedia and then went back to Stein's poem
to find the ways in which it might be 'about' rhubarb, the
vegetable. Clearly Stein's poem is not a source of information about rhubarb, and even more clearly, this poem
does not show me rhubarb (its look, its taste, its smell),
nor does it tell me what rhubarb is doing in *Tender Buttons*
(why not spinach or strawberries?). Is rhubarb a symbol
with a significance beyond its 'vegetableness'? But if it is
a symbol, what does it symbolize? The answer is not in the
poem, nor is it in the cluster of vegetable names that can be
harvested from the rest of *Tender Buttons*. Furthermore, no
matter how cleverly I study the poem 'Rhubarb' for words
or phrases which might possibly have something to do with
the entity rhubarb, I am going to be left with many words
which simply do not satisfy my desire to make this a poem
'about' rhubarb (words like 'susan, ' 'laughable', 'coal' and
'age', for example). In short, although Stein is naming the
things which constitute her domestic environment, she is
not, in fact, reconstituting that environment in her text, at
least not in a way that would make it recognizable to her
reader. She is referring to it, but she is not representing it.
It was out there, but it is not in here.

What is she doing, then, in the poem 'Rhubarb' besides
invoking and inscribing rhubarb, a vegetable which grows
and is harvested, cooked and eaten somewhere outside this
poem? One thing she is doing is playing with words; she
is punning. Coal age = collage. Why this particular pun?
Does she mean to suggest that rhubarb is a name in a
word collage, appearing 'in' the 'fold' between the poems

'Cups' and 'Single Fish'? Is *Tender Buttons* a 'collage' as
Jayne Walker suggests, and is Stein arranging her objects,
foods and rooms like elements in a collage?

Indeed, Stein is preoccupied in the first section of *Tender Buttons* with arrangements and systems (catalogues,
plans, programmes, collections, order). *Tender Buttons* is
itself an arrangement, an attempt at classification. The
entities in Stein's domestic world are divided into three
categories – objects, food and rooms – the text into three
containers for words. (Two of the poems in 'Objects' are
called 'Boxes' and boxes and other containers appear frequently in the poems of this section.) Within 'Objects' and
'Foods' are smaller containers – the poems – one object or
one food inside each poem. The first poem in 'Objects',
which names a kind of container, announces the theme of
arrangement and systematization:

A CARAFE, THAT IS A BLIND GLASS
A kind in glass and a cousin, a spectacle and nothing
strange a single hurt color and an arrangement in a system
to pointing. All this and not ordinary, not unordered in
not resembling. The difference is spreading. (461)

The kinship of the carafe with other objects made of glass,
including spectacles, is 'an arrangement in a system to
pointing'. Even though the carafe is different from spectacles (the carafe is blind, is not a 'seen eye holder' as
Stein puns later), it is similar to spectacles if we point to
the material from which both are made. Glass is the basis
for kinship in this arrangement, in this system. But what if
a carafe were 'all this' but also 'not ordinary' – not part of
a rule or order. Would it be unordered, simply because it
was not resembling others, because it was unique, different?
Suppose we let difference spread. What will we see? We
might see a different kind of arrangement, an arrangement
that pointed to difference, to dissimilarity, to particularity,

to peculiarity (or to the 'pea cooler' as Stein puns in a later poem). That kind of arrangement (the arrangement of a collage) would provide a different kind of spectacle: not the glasses which we use to see the world but the event we look at, a coming together of disparate objects through the juxtaposition of their names in this text.

And what if *Tender Buttons*, the work in which the difference spreads, is that kind of spectacle: not the kind of poem we use, like spectacles, to look at the world and its structure but its own world of wildly colliding word particles. More like 'A Seltzer Bottle' than 'A Carafe':

A SELTZER BOTTLE

Any neglect of many particles to a cracking, any neglect of this makes around it what is lead in color and certainly discolor in silver. The use of this is manifold. Supposing a certain time selected is assured, suppose it is even necessary, suppose no other extract is permitted and no more handling is needed, suppose the rest of the message is mixed with a very long slender needle and even if it could be any black border, supposing all this altogether made a dress and suppose it was actual, suppose the mean way to state it was occasional, if you suppose this in August and even more melodiously, if you suppose this even in the necessary incident of there certainly being no middle in summer and winter, suppose this and an elegant settlement a very elegant settlement is more than of consequence, it is not final and sufficient and substituted. This which was so kindly a present was constant. (466)

'A Carafe' encloses its meaning in an intact and fairly transparent container, much like the object it names; 'A Seltzer Bottle', on the other hand, is a container cracked apart; it has many particles of meaning but suggests no system for arranging them. We cannot read 'A Seltzer Bottle'

with the same ease with which we can read 'A Carafe'.
Though there are blind spots in the carafe – moments of
indeterminacy – interpretations of the poem, and there
are many of them, complement each other and arrive at
approximately the same conclusion, one similar to my own.
'A Seltzer Bottle' has not received any interpretive attention,
at least none that I am aware of; it has been 'neglected'.
What is the use of a seltzer bottle in 'many particles to a
cracking'? What is the use of a poem which does not express
a complete thought, which contains 'mixed' messages?
Stein advises us: 'The use of this' (this seltzer bottle?
this sentence just written? this poem? this whole collection
of tender buttons?) 'is manifold'. Without being confined
to a single use, without having its use (and its meaning)
specified, the seltzer bottle/poem is infinitely adaptable and
useful in unprecedented, unimaginable ways. This ('all
this altogether'), the author's kind 'present', is 'constant'
(faithful, always 'present' to us as we read) regardless of
what becomes of the seltzer bottle in Stein's apartment or
the one in her mind and regardless of the interpretations
that try to mend the break in the glass by elegantly settling
the particles in some 'final and sufficient' system.

Usefulness is a persistent theme of *Tender Buttons*, as
we might expect, since 'usefulness' and 'arrangement'
are interrelated concepts. As Barbara Hernnstein Smith
points out, there is an 'interactive relation between the
classification of an entity and the functions it is expected
or desired to perform'. She continues, 'In perceiving an
object or artifact in terms of some category . . . we implicitly
isolate and foreground certain of its possible functions and
typically refer its value to the extent to which it performs
those functions more or less effectively'.[14] Stein herself
wryly makes a similar observation in 'Rooms': 'A cape is
a cover, a cape is not a cover in summer, a cape is a cover
and the regulation is that there is no such weather'. She
continues, 'In a way there is some use in not mentioning

changing and in establishing the temperature' (502). Stein
wonders what a cape is in summer when it is not in use as
a cover. The rule which classifies the cape as a cover must
ignore such contingencies and focus on a single function of
a cape, the function which defines it and classifies it as a
kind of cover but which does not mention changes in season
or temperature. In this way of thinking, the use of a cape is
limited to one. However, if released from its classification
as a cover, its use becomes manifold: a cape could be a wall
hanging; it could be a decorative throw on a couch; it could
be sewn and stuffed and could become a pillow; spread on
the floor, it could be a rug or a mat for a dog to sleep on;
it could also be waved in the face of a bull. A cape could
be all of these and a cover as well.

In *Tender Buttons*, Stein makes a case for arrangements
which allow for multiple uses of artifacts, be they objects,
words or poems. These arrangements yoke seemingly dis-
similar, disparate entities in a kind of de-classification, 'a
perfectly unprecedented arrangement between old ladies
and mild colds', for example (473). The connection is
'in between' the old ladies, the mild colds. It is the 'and'
which forges the connection. We cannot readily identify
the arrangement which brings these two entities together
because it is unprecedented. It seems to have nothing to do
with the ordinary lexical meaning and syntactical function
of these phrases. Released from the normal cognitive process
signalled by 'and' (the search for similarity and parallelism),
we are free to speculate. Since we have no announced
category to limit our thinking about these entities, our
imagination is brought into play, and our imagination can
transform 'old ladies' and 'mild colds' so that they have
some use other than that normally assigned to them – or,
perhaps, no use at all. Like a parent who gives a child a
large packing crate so that she can transform it into a space
ship, a time machine or a secret cave, so Stein gives us her
containers for our play. We may not get a result from the

play, or, at least, not the kind of result we normally look for from a poem. 'Why is it composed', asks Stein at the end of 'Roast Beef', the first poem in 'Food'. 'The result', she answers, 'the pure result is juice and size and baking and exhibition and nonchalance and sacrifice and volume and a section in division and the surrounding recognition and horticulture and no murmur. This is a result' (481–2). *This* food, a large, juicy roast beef cooking in the oven, its aroma wafting to the desk as Stein works, its presence exhibited by the composition, *this* sentence of unrelated elements drawn together by the force of the 'in betweens', and *this* poem, this perfectly unprecedented arrangement of words – these are the results of the composition. Just as the child will not get to the moon in her wooden space ship, so we should not expect to 'get somewhere' through the poem. We *can* expect to enjoy ourselves while reading the poem, however, if we surrender to and experience the play with language engendered by the juxtaposition of 'old ladies' and 'mild colds', of 'nonchalance' and 'sacrifice', of 'recognition' and 'horticulture'. And, as Stein declares, 'all the pliable succession of surrendering makes an ingenious joy' (484). This too, this 'ingenious joy', is a result.

So then, in *Tender Buttons*, Gertrude Stein is using language to name entities, most of them domestic, and to arrange them in unprecedented configurations which often defy reason but which invite the imagination to play. Since language (her medium) is itself a system, Stein also practices declassification of that system, a subversion of the sentence, that customary grammatical arrangement of words into a meaningful (i.e. useful) unit. By using familiar syntactical structures to define, predicate, suppose, propose, command, question and exemplify, she creates the expectation in the reader that her sentences serve a conventional purpose. However, the content of these Steinian sentences overturns the expectations aroused by their form. For example, when we read 'Nickel, what is nickel, it is originally rid of a cover' (461), we are prepared by the form of the sentence, its kind, to expect a definition of 'nickel'. That is the conventional function of such a sentence. Nonetheless, however we stretch our minds around these words, we cannot make this sentence, so seemingly useful, perform its function. In what universe could 'originally rid of a cover' be said to define 'nickel'?

Even when a definition promises to yield a useful meaning, it does so only fleetingly, as if to tease us, to lead us on in a game of verbal hide-and-seek. For instance, in the definition, 'A recital, what is a recital, it is an organ and use does not strengthen valor, it soothes medicine' (481), the word 'organ' entices us into thinking of organ recitals – a recital as the playing of an instrument (the organ) before an audience. Or stretching further, a recital (the oral kind, as in recitation – of a poem, perhaps) involves another kind of organ, the mouth. Just as we begin to feel like clever readers, having found out some meanings of recital suggested by the tantalizing appearance of 'organ', the word 'organ' slips behind the rest of the sentence, obscured by words that pretend to be completing the definition of 'recital' but that are actually hiding its meaning. Similarly, in the series of sentences – 'A white cup means a wedding. A wet cup means a vacation. A strong cup means an especial regulation. A single cup means a capital arrangement between the drawer and the place that is open' (484) – a reader's expectations, raised by the obvious symbolic association between white and weddings, are undermined somewhat by the odd coupling of 'white' and 'cup'. Still, a white cup could conceivably signify a wedding. However, the subsequent statements, the meanings of which are obscure or nonexistent, mock these kinds of symbolic equations in which an object is taken to 'mean' or symbolize a condition, quality or situation.

This kind of parodying or subversion of rational discourse is a staple of *Tender Buttons*. Thus, we have statements of

causation – 'Why is there education, there is education
because the two tables which are folding are not tied
together with a ribbon' (505) – in which the words that
sit so primly in the subordinate clause are useless to explain
the cause of the phenomenon articulated by the main clause.
And we have if/then propositions in which the conditions
are as baffling as the conclusion they lead to – 'If the red
is rose and there is a gate surrounding it, if inside is let
in and there places change then certainly something is
upright' (464). As readers we are accustomed to exercise
our ingenuity on such statements, to try to use them, but
Tender Buttons repeatedly teases us by withholding meaning
and making our interpretive exercises seem futile.

Similarly, in its performative structures – questions that
demand answers, commands that call for action – *Tender
Buttons* frustrates our normal response to such sentences.
The poem 'Careless Water' ends with this rather urgent
plea for reader participation: 'Supposing a single piece is
a hair supposing more of them are orderly, does that show
that strength, does that show that joint, does that show that
balloon famously. Does it' (470). How are we to answer
these pressing questions if we cannot understand them? And
what are we to do when we are directed, 'Hold the pine, hold
the dark, hold in the rush, make the bottom' (471).

In *Tender Buttons* we are led to see that the value
of language (at least the value of poetic language) is
not to be found in its subordination to a system in
which it must perform a specific signifying function. Of
sentences Stein writes, 'A sentence of a vagueness that
is violence is authority and a mission and stumbling and
also certainly also a prison' (481). In Stein's pun, words
are 'sentenced' to prison. Both 'Objects' and 'Food' begin
with the deconstruction of language systems, and both move
toward the free play of signifiers released from their prisons
of syntax. Syntax becomes increasingly fragmented, and
the hypotactic structures parodied in the earlier poems are

replaced by what Jayne Walker, borrowing from Roman Jakobson, descriptively calls 'word-heaps',[15] like 'black ink best wheel bale brown' (476) and 'Apple plum, carpet steak, seed clam, colored wine, calm seen, cold cream, best shake, potato, potato and no no gold work with pet' (488). The value of these 'word-heaps' is that they allow us (and Stein too) to concentrate on the words themselves, on how they sound and how they look. 'Calm seen' and 'seed clam' appear in the same heap because they look alike; 'cold cream' is there because it sounds like 'calm seen', and 'best shake' because it sounds like 'carpet steak'.

As might be expected, this foregrounding of the phonic constituents of words (letters and their sounds) leads to frequent punning. 'Apple plum' sounds like aplomb; 'carpet steak' like carpet's tack. In other poems we find 'lapse of cuddles' (laps of cuddles) and 'mussed ash' (mustache), 'a no since' (innocence), 'lack use to her' (lackluster), and 'rubbed purr' (rubber). Puns carry over from one poem to another, creating relations among words quite unlike those authorised by syntax. The object 'shoes' gives rise to one such family of words in the poems at the end of 'Objects'. In 'A Little Called Pauline' we find shoes as 'choose wide soles and little spats' (473). The poem 'A Sound' begins 'Elephant beaten with candy and little pops and chews'/lollipops and shoes? The poem 'Shoes' ends with the pun 'shows shine' (474). Similar families of puns inhabit the poems at the end of 'Food'. In one poem we see 'bay leave'/believe, in another 'bay labored'/belaboured, in one 'be where'/beware, in another 'be section'/bisection. In 'Chain-Boats' we have 'blew west carpet'/bluest carpet while in 'Eating' we can read 'belows straight' and hear 'blows straight', just as 'bestow reed' in the final poem of 'Food' can sound like 'be storied', which would explain why 'reed' evolves into 'read' in the course of the poem (493–7). The word 'peculiar' used conventionally in 'Chicken' – 'Pheasant and chicken, chicken is a peculiar bird' (492) – and somewhat conventionally in 'Salmon' – 'It was a peculiar bin a bin fond in beside' (495) – appears disguised as 'pea cooler' in another poem, 'Eating'. In the next poem, also called 'Eating', pea is coupled with pour, which could sound like 'peeper', a pun suggested by the presence of 'as pie' (a spy) in the first 'Eating'. Or perhaps 'pea pour' is a pun on 'paper', suggested by 'a little piece of pay' and 'purred' in the previous poem (494–5). Throughout *Tender Buttons*, words dissolve and reform at a dizzying pace.

These puns depend on the sounds of words, as all puns do, of course, but Stein also indulges in a kind of punning that depends on our looking at the syllabification of words and their spacing on a piece of pay purr, or pea pour, or paper. For example, in the sentence, 'Not a little fit, not a little fit sun sat in shed more mentally' (493), since neither 'sat' nor 'in' are held in place by syntax, they are free to come together in our eye as the two syllables of the word 'satin'. So 'a near ring' can become 'an earring', 'a bout'/about, 'a rested development'/arrested development, 'in sight'/insight, and 'a pease'/appease.

Puns are a way of celebrating the playfulness of language and the many ways in which words can make 'sense'. Words have meaning ('pea', for example, is the name of a vegetable, and Stein uses it 'sensibly' in a 'pea soup' [476]), but they also have sounds and shapes that appeal to our senses – hearing and sight. So Stein can find the words 'Little sales ladies little sales ladies little saddles of mutton. Little sales of leather . . . beautiful beautiful, beautiful beautiful' because, although they do not necessarily make sense, they please the ear and the eye, making a different kind of sense (475).

Puns are also a form of humour, and *Tender Buttons* is full of jokes, many of which are based on puns. We suspect that there are more jokes in *Tender Buttons* than we are aware of since it is in the nature of a joke that some people will not get it, humour being a way of identifying insiders and separating them from outsiders. However, we can become insiders by reading playfully and getting the joke. Sometimes we wonder if we are not seeing more jokes than were actually intended. Still, it is difficult to read 'Leaves in grass' and 'Suppose it is meal' in the same poem and not think of Walt Whitman (*Leaves of Grass*), a poet Stein admired, and Herman Melville (call me Ishmael), a writer she probably read, difficult, that is, not to see this poem as a literary in-joke (492). It is difficult, too, to overlook the scatology in the poem called 'A Brown', which reads in its entirety, 'A brown which is not liquid not more so is relaxed and yet there is a change, a news [anus?] is pressing' (473). And then there are the snatches of nonsense that evoke the jokes of the playground. 'Egg ear nuts' (494) reminds me of a silly song from my own childhood: 'It pays to be egg-er-nut, to be dumb to be stupid to be egg-er-nut, just like me'. The lines, 'Cocoa and clear soup and oranges and oat-meal./Whist bottom whist close, whist clothes, woodling./Cocoa and clear soup and oranges and oat-meal' (496), have the rhythm of a jump rope song and, like such songs, these lines are illogical and thus satisfyingly difficult to memorize and recite, heightening the sense of shared silliness and shared mastery of the knowing participants. A statement like 'it was an extra leaker with a see spoon' creates an alternate universe where there can be logical discourse about silly words like 'see spoon' (495). Of course, we reason, 'a see spoon' (one with holes through which to see) would be an 'extra leaker'.

Up to this point, I have been focusing on Gertrude Stein's writing of *Tender Buttons*, and I have shown how, as a writer, she inscribes objects, deconstructs systems of order and plays with language. But writing is not the only activity happening in *Tender Buttons*. The other activity we witness here is reading. *Tender Buttons* involves three readers: Gertrude Stein, Alice Toklas and me (or you or anyone who opens the books/box in which the tender buttons are kept).

Let us begin with the first reader and the first reading – Gertrude Stein reading her text as she writes it. Most writers erase all evidence of themselves as readers of their own work; that is, they omit from the final work the record of the editing process during which they looked at what they had just written, evaluated it, changed it if necessary and moved on. Stein erases nothing, and in fact, her activity of reading is a source of her writing. Let me offer a few examples. Two poems:

A PETTICOAT
A light white, a disgrace, an ink spot, a rosy charm.

A WAIST
A star glide, a single frantic sullenness, a single financial grass greediness.

Object that is in wood. Hold the pine, hold the dark, hold in the rush, make the bottom.

A piece of crystal. A change, in a change that is remarkable there is no reason to say that there was a time.

A woolen object gilded. A country climb is the best disgrace, a couple of practices any of them in order is so left.

(471–2)

Now, we could imagine that these poems are about a petticoat and a waist (a shirt waist?) though that reading would be difficult to sustain. Or we could imagine that these poems are metaphors for femaleness, especially female sexuality. (In this reading, the rosy charm would be the stain of menstrual blood on a white petticoat, for instance.)[16] Or we could decide that Stein is simply looking at a 'petticoat', 'a star glide' (whatever that might be, perhaps a shooting star outside her window), an 'object that is in wood' (a pine chair with a rush bottom?), 'a piece of crystal' and a 'woolen object gilded' (difficult to picture that) and that she is recording the play of her mind with these objects. I would like to suggest, however, that what is happening in these two poems is that Stein is reading what she has written and that her reading inspires her continued writing. When she reads 'a disgrace' which she has written in the poem 'Petticoat', she thinks of financial disgrace and writes 'financial' in the poem 'A Waist' followed by 'grass', a shadow of the 'grace' from 'disgrace'. Later in 'A Waist', 'a woolen object gilded' probably does not refer to or represent some material object. Rather these words are suggested by other words already written in the poem. Reading 'wood' suggests writing 'woolen', reading 'glide' suggests writing 'gilded'. In a sense the punning and language play I have previously discussed can only come about when a writer reads 'peculiar' and 'pea soup' and thinks and writes 'pea cooler'.

Here are some examples of a different sort of reading/writing:

Cut cut in white, cut in white so lately. (466)

It was a square remain, a square remain not it a bundle, not it a bundle so is a grip, a grip to shed bay leave bay leave draught, bay leave draw cider in low, cider in low and george. George is a mass. (494–5)

Suppose a cod liver a cod liver is an oil, suppose a cod liver oil is tunny, suppose a cod liver oil tunny is pressed suppose a cod liver oil tunny pressed is china. (496–7)

In these examples, we can see how sentences are composed, bit by bit; in other words, we can follow Gertrude Stein's original process of composition. In the first example, she writes 'cut', reads 'cut', and adds 'in white', reads 'cut in white' and adds 'so lately'. Instead of simply presenting us with the *fait accomplit* of the final phrase 'cut in white so lately', Stein preserves the stages of its evolution. In the second example, one part of a phrase is brought forward to initiate a new phrase; thus, from 'It was a square remain', 'a square remain' is read and carried forward to be written into a new phrase, 'a square remain not it a bundle', and so forth. In the third example, the first clause, 'Suppose a cod liver' grows by authorial emendations (a series of readings and writings – re-visions) to end with the clause, 'Suppose a cod liver oil tunny pressed is china'.

As a reader of her own text, Stein maintains a commentary on what she is doing. In other words, *Tender Buttons* contains its own poetics. Like *The Making of Americans* before it, and like many of Stein's works, *Tender Buttons* is a metatext, a text that is self-reflexively focused on the materials and methods of its own composition. Metatextuality in *Tender Buttons* occurs on the most mundane level, as when Stein writes 'easy easy excellent and easy express ec' (494);[17] or 'a window has another spelling, it has "f" all together' (507); or 'a type oh [typo] oh new new not no not knealer' (495); or 'the question does not come before there is a quotation' (462). In these instances, Stein is reflecting on the orthography, transcription and punctuation of her text. At other times, she evaluates and plans the text:

> So then the sound is not obtrusive. Suppose it is obtrusive suppose it is . . . .
> Lovely snipe and tender turn, excellent vapor and slender butter, all the splinter and the trunk, all the poisonous darkening drunk, all the joy in weak success, all the joyful tenderness, all the section and the tea, all the stouter symmetry. (479)

Stein pauses frequently to sum up the effect of her writing, using the demonstrative 'this' to point back to what she has written:

This means a loss a great loss a restitution.   (464)
All this which is a system, which has feeling.   (464)
All this is good.   (479)
All this shows quantity.   (480)
Is this an astonishment.   (484)
This makes it art.   (491)
And this was so charming.   (500)
This astonishes everybody.   (504)
All this is sudden.   (506)

The last section of *Tender Buttons*, 'Rooms', is a reflection on what has been accomplished in 'Objects' and 'Food'. It has many more self-reflexive statements than either of the other two sections, and it is, in its cryptic way, a prolonged explanation and evaluation of the poetics of *Tender Buttons*. In 'Rooms', Stein writes:

> The stamp that is not only torn but also fitting is not any symbol. It suggests nothing. A sack that has no opening suggests more and the loss is not commensurate. The season gliding and the torn hangings receiving mending all this shows an example, it shows the force of sacrifice and likeness and disaster and a reason.
>
> . . .
>
> There was a whole collection made. A damp cloth, an oyster, a single mirror, a mannikin, a student, a silent star, a single spark, a little movement and the bed is made. This shows the disorder, it does, it shows more likeness than anything else, it shows the single mind that directs an apple. (501–2)

And later:

> This is a monster and awkward quite awkward and the little design which is flowered which is not strange and yet has visible writing, this is not shown all the time but

at once, after that it rests where it is and where it is in place. No change is not needed. That does show design. (506)

What does Gertrude Stein think of *Tender Buttons*? In general, she likes what she reads though she recognizes the strangeness of it as well. She sees it as a 'monster', an 'awkward' and disordered text, a text in which there is a disturbance, in which the difference spreads, in which a 'change' has come. In this aberrant text, Gertrude Stein's monster, something is lost, something sacrificed – perhaps a vision of order, the 'harmony' that Stein claims is 'so essential' (500), perhaps the assurance that 'stamps' are 'symbols' and 'suggest' something. The loss is not, however, a cause for mourning. 'No song is sad', she assures herself (500). And she declares, 'All along the tendency to deplore the absence of more has not been authorised' (501).

What has been 'authorised' (and authored) in *Tender Buttons* is a disorderly collection of entities and words which reveals the 'single mind that directs an apple'. The 'visible writing' shows a 'design', not 'all the time' but 'once' in a while. Stein provides the examples, collects the elements, creates the monster, and directs the apple, but it is the readers who must find the design by reading the visible writing. One of these readers, the one who receives the monster directly from Stein's hands, is Alice Toklas, who every day read and typed what had been written. Throughout *Tender Buttons*, this reader is invoked. Coded messages are left for her; private jokes are made for her; veiled sexual fantasies are played out with her in mind. She is addressed more frequently toward the end of each section than at the beginning, as though at the moment of the writer's final departure from the text, the reader is most on her mind.

Alice is invoked by puns on her name: 'a little less', 'a little lace', 'ale less', 'alas', 'eel us', and 'aider' (Ada being one of Stein's alternate names for her 'aider', Alice). Stein addresses Alice directly, in asides – 'A table means does it not my dear it means a whole steadiness' (474), and in poems where Alice's intercession is called for, one at the end of 'Objects' and another at the end of 'Food'. From 'Objects':

THIS IS THIS DRESS, AIDER

Aider, why aider why whow, whow stop touch, aider whow, aider stop the muncher, muncher munchers.

A jack in kill her, a jack in, makes a meadowed king, makes a to let. (476)

And from 'Food':

A CENTRE IN A TABLE

It was a way a day, this made some sum. . . . Suppose a cod liver oil tunny pressed is china . . . and secret with a bestow a bestow reed a reed to be a reed to be, in a reed to be.

Next to me next to a folder, next to a folder some waiter, next to a foldersome waiter and re letter and read her. Read her with her for less. (496–7)

Alice Toklas was Gertrude Stein's lover, and the first poem, which most readers, including myself, find erotically charged, is 'about' loving Alice Toklas. While it is Stein's lover who is addressed in both poems, she is addressed in both as a reader as well as a lover. Lisa Ruddick suggests that 'This Is This Dress Aider' is a morse code distress message – This is distress, m'aidez/Mayday – and that the 'stops' are the signals for sentence breaks.[18] Help me, Stein calls, read my message. The reader, Ada/Alice, can help by completing the text – reading it, transcribing it and enjoying it.

In the second poem, the penultimate lines 'bestow a read' on the 'waiter' (aider/Ada) who will take the 'folder' from the table, and 're letter' (type) it and thereby 'read her' (the writer). The poem ends with a command that encloses two puns: 'Read her with her for less'. As with all commands in *Tender Buttons*, the understood 'you' to whom the command is addressed has multiple reference. Stein is instructing herself (as first reader of the text); she is addressing Alice, her lover, her most ardent reader (this is 'for less'/for Alice), and she is addressing us. She is commanding us and naming us: 'Read her'/reader. As readers, we are with her, Gertrude, and with her, Alice – all of us together, readers of this text.

Far from being the unfriendly, unapproachable text that some find it to be, *Tender Buttons* is an extraordinarily intimate text. It is not so much lure and obstacle as invitation and embrace. Its intimacy does not derive from the fact that it invokes Stein and Toklas's domestic and erotic life since we can never become full participants in that life. Its intimacy comes from our being involved directly in the making of the text. We are drawn into the creative force field of this text, and we experience the writer's constructive energy. When Stein instructs, 'Act so that there is no use in a centre' (498) at the beginning of 'Rooms', she refers to two actions – writing and reading. By writing so that 'there is no use in a centre', Stein has created a text which requires a reading analogous to the writing, a decentered reading, a creative reading, a playful reading. As she acts, so must we. As a writer, she provides us a model for reading. 'The author of all that is in there behind the door' (499). Stein is our teacher, waiting for us behind the door of her studio, the door of her text. When she commands, 'Lecture, lecture and repeat instruction' (483), she is directing herself to lecture us again and again, to repeat her instructions to us. But she is also directing us in how to be instructed. By reading, reading ('lecture' having 'reading' as its root), we repeat instruction. We become wiser in the ways of this text. Alice is the star pupil in this reading school, our surrogate, a reader who loves the writer and the text. By reading as Gertrude writes and as Alice reads, we can learn to embrace *Tender Buttons*. Having been educated in the new way of reading, we can become Stein's playmates, her intimates. The meaning of *Tender Buttons* and its use reside in our experience of it. Rather than giving us a meaning we can remove from *Tender Buttons* and take into our own worlds, Stein invites us to enter hers.

5 Deconstructing Genre: Conversation Plays

Gertrude Stein frequently gave her works generic designations, often using the title or subtitle for that purpose: 'Portrait of Constance Fletcher'; 'Brim Beauvais, a Novelette'; *Lucy Church Amiably: A Novel of Romantic beauty and nature and which Looks Like an Engraving; A Village. Are You Ready Yet Not Yet. A Play in Four Acts;* 'A Poem about Walberg'; and so forth. Though so boldly identified, these works call into question the conventions of the very genre to which they purportedly belong. In chapters 5 and 6 we will be examining some of Gertrude Stein's plays, and we will consider how Stein opposes, mocks, subverts and disrupts the conventions of drama.[1]

Having already observed Stein engaged in similar 'deconstructive' activities, we are by now familiar with her radical stance, and we have some experience with the difficult texts it produces. In her plays, as in her narratives and poems, Stein pushes against the limits that genre imposes on the free play of language and creation. In writing for the theatre, however, Stein encountered the *sine qua non* of drama, that which distinguishes it from other literary genres: the dramatic text, a linguistic construct created by the writer, must become part of an action, a performance by actors before an audience. Writer, actor and audience (the necessary triumvirate of drama) must meet in the theatre, and this eventual meeting requires that the writer of drama accommodate her æsthetic vision to the demands of performance.

Of course, a writer who wishes to experiment with dramatic form unencumbered by thoughts of eventual performance could write closet dramas, but this Stein did not do. She fully intended her plays to be performed. When she began writing plays in 1913, Stein sent several of them to her friend Mabel Dodge, who was well-connected in the New York art world, in the hopes that she would be able to get them produced. Dodge suggested, in a letter, that the plays be published instead. Stein was intransigent: 'No decidedly not. I do *not* want the plays published. They are to be kept to be *played*'.[2] In 1914 when Donald Evans of Claire Marie Press wrote to her asking to publish a volume of her plays, he had been forewarned of her probable refusal. He wrote, 'I should very much like to publish in volume form the plays of yours that Mrs. Dodge has told me about. Will you let me do it? . . . Mr. [Carl] Van Vechten told me he thought you might not wish the plays published before you had them produced here. My bringing out the volume, my dear Miss Stein, would not in any way hurt the producing value; in fact, it would stimulate interest in their production in the theatre'.[3] Stein was not reassured and sent instead the manuscript of *Tender Buttons*. She may have felt, because of promises made by Henry McBride, the art critic of the *New York Sun*, that production was imminent and so, worth waiting for. In August 1913 McBride wrote to Stein as follows regarding the plays she had shown him earlier:

I wanted to read those plays over again and talk with you about them. That man Willis Polk of San Francisco is already returned to Paris. He is Chief of the Architectural Commission for the Fair [The Panama-Pacific International Exposition of 1915], and has some influence in a general way I imagine. I told him that the Fair should stage your plays. . . . To do the gentleman justice, I must say, his eyes sparkled at the idea. . . . In the meantime, I still think they should be done next winter in New York, and if they are done, I hope I shall be allowed to help. If you see anything in the Fair, let me know and I'll nab Polk. He gave me the idea that the San Franciscans would love to be up to date or a little ahead of it, if possible.[4]

Nothing ever came of these promises and the plays in question were eventually published in 1922 in *Geography and Plays* without having been produced.

Stein objected not only to the idea of her plays as closet dramas, available only in print, but also to the idea that they were esoteric pieces suitable only for minimal staging in the context of a literary salon or art society. In 1944 and 1945 Stein made various efforts to have *Yes Is For a Very Young Man* produced, even translating it into French for a proposed production at the American Army University at Biarritz, under her supervision. However, she abruptly withdrew her play from this production because, as Alice Toklas explained in a letter to Carl Van Vechten, she objected to a 'workshop performance', that is a production without scenery and to a 'hand-picked audience'.[5]

Although Stein started writing plays in 1913, it wasn't until 1934 that her wish to have her plays performed was gratified. *Four Saints in Three Acts*, the play Stein wrote as a libretto for the American composer Virgil Thomson, opened in Hartford, Connecticut on 8 February 1934, and later that month on Broadway for a run of forty-eight performances. It met with a warm, if somewhat puzzled reception from audiences and critics. Most who saw it agreed that Virgil Thomson's music helped them to accept and even enjoy the enigmatic Stein libretto, which was described most often as nonsense, albeit engaging nonsense.

In fact, performances of Stein's plays have often had some sort of musical accompaniment or scoring, as though the producer hoped through music to make the text more palatable to audiences. Even with musical accompaniment, however, there have been few productions of Stein's plays in the years since 1934. The most noteworthy of these was the 1951 Living Theatre production of *Doctor Faustus Lights the Lights* (director Judith Malina), of which Julian Beck writes, 'We [the members of the Living Theatre] wanted to do some of her [Stein's] work and wanted to open the Living Theatre with *Doctor Faustus Lights the Lights* because it was like a manifesto and would always stand at the head of our work saying take the clue from this'.[6] More recently, in 1982, *Doctor Faustus Lights the Lights* was staged in Berlin by director Richard Foreman, whose own plays for his Ontological-Hysteric Theatre demonstrate Stein's influence. Acknowledging his debt to Stein, Foreman has said, 'I have always felt that Gertrude Stein is the major literary figure of the twentieth century . . . [she] obviously was doing all kinds of things we haven't even caught up to yet'.[7] During the sixties, another New York avant-garde theatre company, the Judson Poets' Theatre, mounted four of Stein's plays under the direction of Lawrence Kornfeld, with Al Carmines as composer. By and large, however, Stein's plays have found few sympathetic directors and, when produced, have failed to reach mainstream audiences.

I believe that Stein's plays have been neglected because they are, to a great degree, anti-theatrical. That is, while Stein intends her plays to be performed and while she engages and experiments with the conventions that shape a play text for performance (act/scene divisions, character ascriptions, scene setting, the development of character, the unfolding of an action), she is writing plays that render performance problematic.

In the theatre, language, the writer's medium, must coexist with other competing 'languages' – gesture, scenic space, action. Dramatic texts are shaped by considerations of these other languages, especially action. Keir Elam has written that 'the primary allegiance of language in the drama' is to the 'course of events',[8] and Jindřich Honzl states that the interrelatedness of word and act is an 'enduring law of theatrical creativity and perception'.[9] Language is not necessarily subordinate to action, but a poet writing for the theatre must attempt to achieve a balance between word and act. The dramatic text must anticipate its eventual performance, and the writer for the theatre usually seeks a compromise between textual principles and theatrical principles. The resulting text facilitates its own performance. Gertrude Stein was not interested in such a compromise. Her texts seem to resist the very performance they instigate. Stein attempts to oppose the physicality of performance, to stop the driving force of action and to prevent the written text, the writer's words, from being subsumed by the other elements of the performance event.

II

The plays which Stein wrote between 1913 and 1919 are sometimes referred to as dialogues; I call them 'conversations' in order to emphasise the fact that although they present the alternating addresses and responses of speaking partners, the resulting conversation differs profoundly from conventional dramatic dialogue. Conventional dramatic dialogue calls into existence a non-linguistic world, a world of objects, actions and actors, and this physical world, set in motion by the dialogue, then affects its shape, direction and content. Stein's conversation plays suggest that there is no non-linguistic world, that the only 'event' taking place in the world of the play is speech. All other components of theatrical art seem to drop away, and we are left with language and with the drama inherent in language. The drama in Stein's conversation plays is in speech acts and the relationships they establish. It is in the way the speakers collaborate through language. It is in the momentum of language, the rhythms of social discourse. It is in the suggestiveness of words, how they can trigger a thought and change the subject of the conversation.

In conventional drama, dialogue is also meant to reveal character and to convey a plot line (or at least to introduce and to resolve conflict). In Stein's conversation plays, dialogue does not perform these conventional functions. Stein said that her 'idea' in writing plays was 'to express . . . each one being that one and there being a number of them knowing each other . . . without telling what happened, in short to make a play the essence of what happened' (LIA 119). Although she wanted her plays to be the 'essence of what happened', she did not want them to tell stories. In a sense, of course, no play 'tells' a story. Rather, the language of the play is the story; as it is spoken or read, the dialogue creates the world of the play and the state of affairs in that world, or, as Stein put it, the dialogue is 'what made what happened be what it was' (LIA 122). That is why drama has been considered the most mimetic mode – because in it fictive language comes as close as it ever can to being a present action with immediate consequences, rather than a representation, after the fact, of non-linguistic actions, states and objects.

However, the mimetic theory of drama rests on a fallacy. In fact, the 'story' precedes and shapes the dialogue of even, and perhaps especially, the most natural-seeming, the most mimetic plays. Like poetry, plays are not natural but fictive utterances.[10] Dramatic dialogue is not primary and constitutive, but secondary and derivative, not a natural phenomenon but an artificial one. However, the pretense of naturalness is at the heart of dramatic mimesis; Stein's conversation plays at once engage in and expose this pretense. They sound much like real conversations and not at all like conventional dramatic dialogue, thereby revealing the ways in which dramatic dialogue is not like ordinary discourse.

In order for a play text to be the essence of what happened, which is what Stein hoped her plays would be, 'what happened' must be a linguistic event, a speech act, since, with respect to other kinds of events and acts (for example, a narrative event, like two people meeting on a train, or a performance event, like an actor falling down), language can only be a report or a response, but not the thing itself. Stein's conversation plays appear to be written records of speech acts, and nothing more. These conversations are not shaped by a preconceived plot, nor do they conform to a generically approved structure such as the dramatic arc of conflict and resolution. They are not windows onto a non-linguistic world. They are themselves the world – a world of conversations without stories.

A short play from this period, *Can You See the Name*, is one such conversation without a story:

CAN YOU SEE THE NAME

The name that I see is Howard.
Yes.
And the water that I see is the sea.
Yes.
And the land is the island.   5
Yes.
And the weather.
And the weather.
Cold
Indeed.   10
And the cause.
The cause of what.
The cause of lust.
Lust is not a name.
Indeed not.   15

And bushes.
Can you fear bushes.
Not I.
You mean you are braver.
Braver and braver.   20
What is the meaning of current.
Current topics.
Yes and then.
And then colors.
Green colors.   25
Lord Melbourne says blue is unlucky.
This is fear.
When can you see us.
Whenever I look.
And when are you careful.   30
I am very careful to smile.
Then we have our way.
Indeed you do and we wish it.
We are glad of your wishes.
It is not difficult to drive.   35
Curtain let us.
We do
We will.
Thank you so much.
You learnt that before.   40
I learn it again.
Do you know the difference in authors.[11]

Despite its brevity, *Can You See the Name* is typical in
all other ways of the longer conversation plays, most of
which were published in *Geography and Plays*. In *Can
You See the Name*, as in all of Stein's conversation plays,
language is given prominence over, indeed, almost exists
without the other components of theatrical art – objects,
action, actors – which we are used to having suggested or
called for in the dramatic text. We notice immediately,

for example, the absence of a side text; there are no stage directions, not even character ascriptions in this play. The more side text a play has, the more lines of the text will have to be eliminated from performance, leaving gaps in the continuity of meaning or gaps in dramatic structure. These gaps will be filled with action and with the dramatic space (including scenic set and stage). Therefore, the more side text the playwright uses, the more important action, actors and space become, and, conversely, the less side text, the less important these elements are. In a play without side text, the language is thus foregrounded.

The immediate effect of this foregrounding is to make the experience of silently reading this play similar in one respect to the experience of hearing it read aloud. That is, for the reader of the play, as for the auditor, all information about the objective world of the play must come from the conversation. And if this particular conversation were to be staged, the stage would very likely be empty except for the speakers since conversation here seems to exist in a void, a space without objects and actions.

In staging a conventional play, we can look not only to its stage directions but also to its dialogue for the objects, conditions, actions and actors we are to realize in the theatre. Looking at *Can You See the Name* for 'objects' we find a name, a sea, an island, bushes, current topics, the color green, the color blue, wishes, a curtain. As for conditions, we have cold weather, lust, fear, bravery, carefulness, gladness, ease, difference. For actors, besides the speakers (of which we may have two or more), we have a 'Howard', a 'Lord Melbourne', and some 'authors'. What do these actors do? Some of them certainly talk, and when they talk, they use the verbs 'to look', 'to see', 'to smile', 'to have one's way', 'to drive', 'to learn', and 'to know'. Nevertheless, beyond the scene setting of the first section, the physical, objective, active world of the play is difficult to imagine because the objects, conditions, actors and actions I have named, which are introduced as objects of discourse, remain forever in the world of discourse.

Stein's very title is emblematic of the way in which her play functions as an autonomous world of discourse without apparent connection to the world beyond the words. Ordinarily a play's title will evoke a central object, action or condition that underlies all the talk of the play: *The Wild Duck*, *Waiting for Godot*, *Six Characters in Search of an Author* and so forth. But *Can You See the Name*, while it occupies the position of a title, is actually a line of the discourse, a question answered by the very first line: 'The name that I see is Howard'. This incorporation of the title into the conversation is a common device in Stein's conversation plays.

It is not because of Stein's idiosyncratic use of titles alone that her plays are closed systems of discourse. It is also because of the words of the plays, specifically the nouns and verbs. It is through nouns and verbs, after all, that the words of a play can specify its world. Stein's words themselves are sufficiently concrete, one would think, to fulfil the normal function of words in a play. The difference between Stein's play language and ordinary play language rests not in the kinds of words she chooses but in her use of them.

As in an ordinary play, the nouns in Stein's conversation plays are referential. So in line 3 of *Can You See the Name*, 'And the water that I see is the sea', the noun 'water' refers to an actual body of water which can be observed and which can be labelled with another noun, the near synonym 'sea'. But the noun 'sea' is not only, nor most importantly, the sign of an object (a body of water) or of an event (looking at the body of water). It is itself both object and event. After all, water, the object, is first suggested in the conversation by the word 'see' in the title and in line 1 (an object itself, a printed word on the page) which when spoken (when, that is, it becomes eventful) suggests its homonym 'sea' which brings the object, the body of water, to mind. In

other words, the noun 'sea' has an undeniable connection
to a physical entity, but its position and presentation in the
conversation attenuate and de-emphasise its referentiality
and emphasise instead its existence as a word suggested
by another word which sounds the same but is spelled
differently. In short, our attention is focused on phonology
and orthography, not on meaning.[12]

With proper nouns, too, referentiality is de-emphasised.
'Howard' may refer to a person, but in the world of this
play, 'Howard' is only a name that we can see, an object
in the written text, an entity, not a referent. The name
'Lord Melbourne', on the other hand, is clearly referring
to someone, but this someone exists in the world of the
play only as a topic of conversation, a name spoken and
spoken about, part of a speech act, but not himself an actor.
Stein's proper names and her nouns force us to concentrate
on language, not to look through it as as though it were
transparent.

Like her nouns, Stein's verbs function to keep the objects
of discourse in the world of discourse. An inventory of
Stein's verbs as they occur throughout the conversation
plays helps to explain how they accomplish this. Of the
thirty verbs in *Can You See the Name*, for example, one-third
are forms of the verb 'to be'. This ratio holds true in
most of the conversation plays. Stein also favors verbs
which express preference – 'care for', 'like' and 'wish',
for instance – or which express a mental activity – 'know',
'remember', 'learn', 'understand', 'recollect' and 'forget'.
These types of verbs do not suggest non-linguistic actions
which might accompany the conversation in which they
occur. The most common verbs in the conversation plays
are metalingual verbs: 'mean', 'hear', 'explain', 'mention',
'speak', 'say', 'assure', 'ask', 'agree', 'call', 'contradict',
'promise', 'pronounce' and 'spell'. Thus, the most common activities in these plays are linguistic activities. All of
these linguistic activities occur within the primary activity,

conversation. When conversation is about language and language-making activities, language becomes an object of interest in its own right and is, itself, the object of discourse.

True action verbs, when they occur in *Can You See the Name*, are presented in inactive forms: in the infinitive – 'It is not difficult to drive' (l. 31); 'I am very careful to smile' (l. 35); or with the auxiliary 'can' – 'Can you fear bushes' (l. 17); 'When can you see us' (l. 28) – both verb forms suggesting the possibility of action but not action itself. Action verbs presented actively are primarily presented as responses to questions, not as responses to actions that have just occurred in the world of the play. For example: 'Can You See the Name/The name that I see is Howard' (l. 1); 'When can you see us./Whenever I look' (ll. 28–9). Action exists most frequently, then, outside the world of the play and exists at all only because it is reported in the 'here and now' of the conversation.

In addition to disrupting the normal reference of dramatic language to objects, people and actions outside the world of discourse, Stein's conversation plays subvert the conventional form of dramatic dialogue, which is usually distinguished from normal discourse by a high degree of co-referentiality, an interconnectedness of the objects of discourse.[13] Ordinarily, with each appearance in a play text, by a process of accretion, a word becomes something more than the signifying sequence of letters it was in its first appearance as an object of discourse. For example, the first time Blanche Dubois mentions Belle Reve in Tennessee Williams's play *A Streetcar Named Desire*, the words are simply letters on a page, sounds in the air. That they name a place is all we know from the context in which we first read or hear them. As we move through the play, however, the name gathers significance by its repeated use in the speech of the characters. Around it grows a matrix of symbolic meaning; finally, of course,

'Belle Reve' is much more than two words performing a nominative function in the discourse of the characters in the play. This process by which a word acquires attributes beyond its lexical meaning, its grammatical function, its spelling and its pronunciation does not take place in Stein's conversation plays. In some plays this is because a word, once introduced, may never reappear. Even when a word appears repeatedly, its recurrences serve to fragment the text rather than to join its parts. No connection is made between separate occurrences. The repeated words and phrases do not recur at regular intervals, or in the same or similar contexts or with the same or similar reference. Instead of unifying the whole, such repetition interrupts the ongoing flow of the whole, constantly sending the listener back to a new beginning. We never see in Stein's conversation plays the progressive construction of a coherent text or a coherent world.

In the social discourse recorded in *Can You See the Name*, the speaking partners behave as collaborators in the clarification of meaning and the amplification of information. Yet their conversation is not clear and informative for the reader/auditor's purposes because it has the characteristics of ordinary social discourse – 'digression, redundancies, non sequiturs, sudden changes of topic and . . . an overall inconclusiveness' – characteristics which make ordinary discourse much less clear and informative than dramatic dialogue.[14] In *Can You See the Name* the speakers change topic abruptly in lines 13, 16, 21, 24, 27, 28, 30, 35, 36, 40 and 42. Almost every change of topic is a non sequitur; there is no strategic organization at work in this conversation. Some topics recur: 'fear', introduced in line 17, is reintroduced in line 27; 'seeing', the topic which initiates the conversation, appears again in line 28. But these repetitions do nothing to develop the topic. They contribute, in fact, to the overall inconclusiveness and fragmentation of this conversation which begins and ends with a question. Despite the confusion such a conversation causes the reader/auditor, the speakers appear to understand each other quite well. This play, then, is truly a closed world, one constituted as if there were no outside observers. Compared to this play, so-called 'realistic' drama with its invisible fourth wall can be seen more clearly as the artifact it is, an artifact constructed from the materials of dialogic exchange which are then strategically manipulated to inform and to affect the eventual audience at the performance. Stein's plays subvert the informational and affective function of dramatic dialogue because Stein imposes no temporal ordering and no action structure on her conversations. They are dialogic exchanges, but in them, the give and take of dialogue is not shaped by considerations of plot, performance or even character.

The participants in this social discourse are not at all like the characters who emerge from most dramatic dialogue. In the first place, the lines of dialogue are undifferentiated from speaker to speaker, leading some to conclude, as Richard Bridgman does, that they issue 'from a single sensibility'.[15] Of course, all the words in any play text issue from a single sensibility, the dramatist's, but ordinarily we expect the dramatist to manipulate language so that it appears to issue from several sensibilities since one of the chief functions of dramatic dialogue is to create characters which actors can then impersonate. Like all plays, Stein's are imagined as being uttered by more than one speaker. The absence of idiosyncracies differentiating one speaker from the next points to the absence, not of speakers, but of characters. Language is foregrounded and characters, like objects, conditions and actions, are de-emphasised.

Even when speakers are named, as they are in a few of the conversation plays and even when they give us information about themselves, they are not characters. Susanne Langer has stated that 'a character [in a play] stands before us as a coherent whole'.[16] This Stein's speakers never do. They are not characterized, either by habits of speech or through coherent portrayal.

Let us imagine for a moment what would happen to these play texts in performance.[17] In performance the language of the play is given voice. If the play text is a conversation, then that conversation will be performed by speakers. Once language becomes attached to living people, the playwright loses control of it as a medium. Speech becomes identified with the individual who utters it. No matter how assiduously the playwright avoids characterization, speech is a characterizing act. By imitating conversation and by foregrounding it, Stein was automatically creating an opportunity for the speaker to mimic a living person and through the tone, intensity and timbre of his voice to invest that person with character. Since actors have bodies as well as voices, they will act as well as speak. At the very least an actor will normally underline speech with accessory movement, gestures and the like.

A performance which is true to the text of these plays will minimize characterization and action. Nonetheless, in even the most impersonal and static performance, the very components of theatrical art which Stein's plays eliminate or demote can re-enter the play through the intermediary of the actor. Because Stein's medium is conversation, the autonomy and primacy of language will inevitably be compromised in performance, no matter how faithful that performance is to the written text. In the plays Stein wrote after 1919, the conflict between the written play text and the performance text (where all the elements that the written text eliminated may become reinstated) replaces conversation as the focus of the plays and as the source of their dramatic tension.

6 Reconstructing Genre: Lang-scapes and Schizologues

I Lang-scape Plays: 1920–27

The plays written between 1920 and 1927, which are collected in *Operas and Plays* and *Last Operas and Plays*, Gertrude Stein called landscapes. I have adapted rather than adopted her term partly because there is no evidence that the desire to create verbal landscapes guided her in the writing of these plays. She first called her plays 'landscapes' in her 1935 lecture 'Plays', well after most of them had been written. Moreover, 'landscape' is less than satisfactory as a descriptive designation of these plays because it suggests that they represent, evoke or in some manner correspond to a specific place (an idea Stein fosters by her claim that they were inspired by the countryside around Bilignin, France). In fact, the plays are not about Bilignin or any other place. Rather, they are about language and its relationship to the performance event; they are about writing for the theatre, thus my alteration of the prefix – from 'land' to 'lang' – to give some sense of the true subject of these plays. Although 'landscape' does not adequately describe the plays, I did not wish to abandon the term entirely, for I find 'landscape' a suggestive metaphor for these plays. I therefore wanted to retain some trace of it.

The metaphoric connection between landscape and theatre has a long tradition, embodied most neatly in the word 'scene' with its application to both worlds. In the essay

'Thought and Landscape', Yi-Fu Tuan defines landscape as a 'space in which people *act*', or '*scenery* for people to contemplate' (emphasis added).[1] In the same spirit, but centuries earlier, 'theatre' was a word commonly used in the titles of books of travel and geographic description. On the other side of the metaphoric field, dramatists of the 16th and 17th century made frequent use of the *theatrum mundi* topos, and during the same period the Italians developed the proscenium stage which borrowed its vanishing point perspective and disposition of loci in space from landscape painting. In choosing this metaphor for her own plays, then, Stein reminds us of a centuries-old theatrical convention. Although Stein's plays are not in themselves landscapes, not the verbal depiction or evocation of a scene, they are like landscapes. The similitude lies in Stein's use of language. About the similarity between landscape and language, John Jakle writes, 'Landscapes comprise a syntax. Not only do objects have meaning like words, but objects relate spatially not unlike a grammatical structure. Objects in the environment can have collective meaning given the visual relationships of place'.[2] Stein treats her words as though they are material objects related to each other spatially, that is, visually on the page and sonorously in the air. Her language assumes a materiality equal in presence to the materiality of the other elements of the performance event.

Furthermore, the effect of these plays on our perception of their performance is similar to the effect of landscape on our perception of our environment. Originally an Anglo-Saxon word which meant simply a tract of land, 'landscape' fell out of use until it was revived by Dutch painters in 1600 to refer to their representations of a scene. 'Landscape' in its modern usage, then, described first a kind of painting and only later the view or prospect itself. The word as a designation of something in the environment, the view we see, would always suggest artfulness. Landscape is always a composition, whether created as such by a landscape architect or organized that way by the eye of the perceiver, trained by art to compose the view. A word like 'landscape' which suggests the power of art to alter perception has a wonderful resonance when applied to Stein's plays because their structure, their 'scape', alters the normal course of the theatre event. By opposing the dynamism of actor and action, Stein's plays create a kind of verbal stasis within theatre time, much as a landscape painting frames and freezes a visual moment in natural time or as a 'real' landscape interferes with the process of nature. Within this stasis, Stein represents an event not normally represented in the theatre: the writing of the play.

In the lang-scape plays written between 1920 and 1923, the words of the play are presented first and foremost as visible objects, the writer's materials. How they look on the page (spelling, capitalization, physical placement) and how they relate to each other (punctuation and syntax) determine how the theatre event will be constituted. Thus Stein asserts the spatiality of words and the primacy of the written text (both side text and main text) over the performance text. Far from making her written text the transparent instrument of theatrical realization, she makes it a material presence whose existence and contours are the subject of debate and discussion within the play. The actors in these plays are never allowed to forget that their own material existence depends upon a particular reading of the written text. The theatre event of which a Stein play is a part really begins with that reading, with the encounter between enactor (producer, director or actor) and text. Lawrence Kornfeld, the director of four of Stein's plays, has described his and his actors' encounters with Stein's texts:

For me the real play is the process. . . . Gertrude Stein's plays can be very boring if the director tries to make them

all about the words of ideas, or the words of love, or the
words of painting or the words about words. This is
wrong. The director must fight the plays and then he
will find out what the words mean, not what the words
are about. Only Gertrude Stein knew what the words
were about; we can manage to hear what they mean if
we put up a good fight. Only Gertrude Stein cared what
the words were about and maybe some of her friends for
gossip cared, but I only care about what they will mean
after we all fight over them.[3]

Examining a representative play from the period, we can
see how a Stein play engages its enactors in a 'fight' as they
try to move from reading to enactment. The play in question
is *A List* (1923), a play which seems to be about making a
list of the characters in the play. In a conventional play in
which the side text exists to facilitate enactment, each name
in the side text signifies a new 'character' which an actor
will then impersonate in performance. The establishment
of a character list is thus a fairly straightforward affair (often
done for the actors by the playwright in a list that precedes
the first act of the play). By contrast, the side text in *A List*
presents an immediate challenge. In this play, which Stein
teasingly calls *A List*, a list of characters is not, in fact,
very easy to generate.

 In Stein's notational system a name followed by a period
is a character speaking:

    Martha.   not interesting.

Two names joined by 'and' signifies two characters speaking
in unison:

    Martha
      and   Included.
    Maryas.

Three names, three characters:

Mabel	
Martha	Various re-agents make me see
and	victoriously.
Maryas.	

What are we to make, then, of this configuration?

Mabel	
Martha	Susan Mabel Martha and Susan, Mabel
and	and Martha and a father. There was
Mabel	no sinking there, there where there was
and	no placid carrier.
Martha.	(O&P 89)

Do we have two characters, Mabel and Martha, or three characters, Mabel Martha, and Mabel, and Martha? We have only two names after all, but the usual correspondence between name and person is disrupted here by the arrangement of the names and their relationship via the connector 'and'. The words spoken by this group of characters further emphasise the effect of syntax on meaning. When they say 'Susan Mabel Martha and Susan, Mabel and Martha' the same names appear on both sides of that first 'and'. In performance this line would sound like the repetition of names referring to the same people. But the written text gives us different information because of the existence of the comma. (The inclusion of 'and' between 'Mabel' and 'Martha' also alters the significance of the three names.) We cannot 'recognize it by the name' as one of the characters later challenges us to do, partly because the meaning of a name – or of any word – can be altered by its syntactical placement, not only within a sentence or a phrase, but also within the play.[4]

The title of this play, for example, is 'A List'. This configuration of words means that there is only one list unless, as happens halfway into the play, we encounter the same words arranged like this:

LIST A

By a syntactical reversal, the single list becomes the first of a number of lists – but only in the side text – for within the main text (the text to be spoken) the characters continue to refer exclusively to 'a list'. Meaning then depends on where words (names) appear within the grammar of the sentence and within the 'grammar' of the text.

When the characters begin referring to a second list, the existence of more than a single list enters the world of the main text. Yet the main text stops with a second list, while the side text gives us 'THIRD LIST', 'FOURTH LIST', 'LIST FIVE', and 'A LAST LIST'. Six lists in all, or seven if we count the first list announced by the title of the play, but six or seven only within that part of the composition that is the side text, six or seven lists only for the reader not for the spectator or listener. If we are to recognize it by the name, our recognition will depend upon what field of composition we are attending to. If we want to recognize all of 'it' in a play, we must look at the written text as well as listen to the spoken text.

Moreover, we must look at the written text because only there can we see the words spelled out for us. Through an abundance of homophones, homonyms and puns, Stein demonstrates how difficult it is to get a fix on the material world of the play without first getting a fix on the material of the play – those letters out of which spelling makes recognizable names. Only when we can see the words can we understand what we are hearing in performance.

Take, for example, the character names, 'Maryas' and 'Marius'. As written they are distinguishable, and so, in the side text, they seem to stand for two separate characters (except when they combine as in the 'Mabel

Martha' mode discussed above). But Maryas and Marius are near homophones, and when spoken they are barely distinguishable. If both names are pronounced the same, what then becomes of the two characters signalled by the names? This is a question which naturally concerns not only the eventual actors but the 'characters' themselves.[5] Marius asks, 'How do you spell Marius', because his very existence depends on the spelling of his name in the written text (O&P 96). In the following exchange the characters meditate on the difference between speaking and spelling:

Maryas and Martha.	More Maryas and more Martha.
Maryas and Martha.	More Martha and more Maryas.
Martha and Maryas.	More and more and more Martha and more Maryas.
Marius.	It is spoken of in that way.
Mabel.	It is spoken of in that way.
Marius and Mabel.	It is spoken in that way and it is spoken of in that way.
Marius and Mabel.	It is spoken of in that way.
Mabel.	I speak of it in that way.
Marius.	I have spoken of it in that way and I speak it in that way. I have spoken of it in that way.
Mabel.	I speak of it in that way.
Mabel.	Spelled in this way.
Marius.	Spelled in that way.

Mabel.   Spelled in this way and spelled in that way
                    and spoken of in this way and spoken of
                    in that way and spoken in this way.

                                                        (O&P 93)

The other characters speak of 'Maryas', but when they
speak of him, the names which are spelled in this
way – 'Maryas' – and in that way – 'Marius' – might be
spoken in only one way. When we hear the words in
performance we may hear only one name unless the actors
take great care to pronounce the two names differently.
We must therefore attend to the written text in order to
compose an accurate list of characters.

That the written text is more reliable than the performance text as a key to exactly what is said and what is
seen is further emphasised by the appearance of other
homophones within the main text. For example, Maryas
poses the following number puzzle:

> Sixteen if sixteen carry four, four more, if five more carry
> four for more if four more carry four, if four carry fifty
> more, if four more five hundred and four and for more
> than that, and four more than eighty four. Four more
> can carry sixteen if you please if it is acceptable.

                                                        (O&P 91)

When we hear the word 'four', we will correctly assume
because of its context that we are hearing the particular
sequence of letters that signifies the number '4'. However,
we will also assume, this time incorrectly, that 'for' means
the number '4'. Only the written text can set us straight.

Names, however, are not like the word 'for'. Names (and
by extension, nouns) have a correspondence to something
in the material world. (Names and nouns can also stand
for ideas and abstractions, but Stein is more concerned
here with the relationship between a name and an object).
Maryas Mabel and Martin ask, 'How are you known', and

answer, 'You are known by your name and your share' (O&P 102). Or as Martha later puts it, 'Carrots and artichokes marguerites and roses. If you can repeat it and somebody chose it, somebody shows it, somebody knows it. If you can repeat and somebody knows it' (O&P 103). Objects are known by their names and by their 'share', their unique place in the material world. The name is that which was chosen to represent a unique carrot, a particular rose. We repeat the name and each time we do 'carrot' is shown and carrot is known. This is a very generalized carrot, not the first one seen when someone chose the name for it. The name is not exactly the same thing as each and every carrot that has a share in the material universe, but the name is one way to recognize the existence of carrot.

So it is when we make a list; the names on it have a direct correspondence to items with a share in the world. Either we make a list of what we see – a list of the contents of a box, for instance, in which case we write down a name for each item we pull out of the box. Or we make a list of what we wish to see or what we believe we could eventually see – a shopping list, for example, in which case we are certain that for each name we write down there exists an item that can be procured by the person who takes the shopping list to the appropriate place.

This is not exactly the situation with a character list, however. The names on a character list do not correspond to anything or anyone preexisting in the material world. The names are inventions of the dramatist which correspond to imagined beings who exist only in the private world of the dramatist's mind. (This is even true, to a certain extent, of characters with the names of historical personages.) To make a list of characters, then, we must look to the dramatist, not to the visible world.

The problem of making such a list in *A List* is first posed by Martha as a meditation which becomes a leitmotif of the play:

Martha.   If four are sitting at a table and one of
           them is lying upon it it does not make any
           difference. If bread and pomegranates are on
           a table and four are sitting at the table and
           one of them is leaning upon it it does not
           make any difference.

Martha.   It does not make any difference if four are
           seated at a table and one is leaning upon
           it. (O&P 92)

Bread and pomegranates, having been named and having
names which correspond to real objects, can be said without
hesitation to be on the table. But what can be said for certain
about the people sitting at the table? Without names they
are at the mercy of syntax. One of them can appear and
disappear with the shifting of a few words. If we say, 'four
are sitting at the table and one of them is leaning upon
it', we are speaking of four people, but if we eliminate the
phrase 'of them' and say that four are seated and one is
leaning, we may now be speaking of either four or five
people. If Stein had written unequivocally, 'Martha and
Mabel and Martin and Marius are sitting at the table and
Mary is leaning upon it', we would know how many people
are at the table.

Or would we? 'Yes and know' to borrow a line from
the play. As we have seen, even when we move out
into the side text, a space full of names, we meet with
a writer who teases us with her homophones and her
syntactical maneuvers, teases us with the essentially self-
contained world of the written text where words exist
not as pointers but as objects in a composition. In this
play, as Martha says, ' . . . the pansy is a bird as well
as a flower rice is a bird as well as a plant, cuckoo is
a flower as well as a bird' (O&P 91). Whatever correspondence the words have to a material world beyond the
play, that correspondence is not the only, and certainly

not the most important reason for their presence in the play.

The experience Lawrence Kornfeld and his actors have had with Stein's plays is an experience I believe Stein intended them to have. Stein's language does not represent something else. It simply exhibits itself. The enactor's first act must be to experience the language and not to read into it a meaning that the text does not itself present. By opposing the processes an enactor would normally go through to dissolve, transform, overwhelm, menace or subordinate the written text in order to create the performance text, Stein asserts the substantiality of her written text and makes it an active participant, as it were, in the process of its own enactment.

Let us suppose, now, that an enactor has met Stein's challenge and has created from the written text of *A List* a performance text that is now to be exhibited to an audience. Even in the performance text, language is made conspicuous. What is conspicuous in the performance of *A List* (or what would be conspicuous – the play has not, to my knowledge, been performed) is not, of course, the way words look but the way words sound. In *A List* the speeches of characters are not connected conversationally, but chorally. These characters seldom use language as an instrument of communication. Rather than responding to what the words mean, they simply respond to the words. They repeat them, or they repeat them with slight variations. They match the sounds of words already spoken with similar sounds, like poets completing each other's poems. They free associate in a world where words suggest other words. In a performance of this play, the æsthetic qualities of language would be insistent, making it difficult for us to attend to other qualities like instrumentality and reference. We might try to draw meaning from the words, but our attention to them as signifiers would be distracted by our awareness of them as objects 'filling' the air of the theatre as sound can fill a room. By giving prominence to language sounds, Stein is calling attention to the materials from which the play has been constructed. She is making opaque that which is usually transparent. By subverting the conventional role of dramatic language in this way, Stein is making the spectator attend to the materiality of language, to its existence as an æsthetic object. The foregrounding of language in the theatre is a difficult enterprise. As a writer with an idiosyncratic and privatized semiotic system, Stein would have had to face the public character of language in the theatre. In the public forum of the theatre, private meanings are lost; self-reflexive games played with written words are meaningless. One is left simply with sound – signifying nothing. Or with silence. It is impossible to say whether or not Stein realized in 1923 the limitations of linguistic free play in a performance text. The fact is, though, that Stein wrote no plays from 1924 to 1927.

Stein returned to writing for the theatre in 1927 when Virgil Thomson, then living in Paris, commissioned her to write an opera.[6] Thomson and Stein agreed that the opera would be about the lives of working artists as symbolized by the lives of saints. They chose Saint Teresa (Stein and Toklas's favourite saint)[7] and Saint Ignatius Loyola as the principle saints in order to provide the opera with a male and female lead. Stein adhered generally to the specification of saints as characters, but the play is less about the working lives of artists (or the lives of saints) than it is about an artist at work; the artist is Gertrude Stein and her work is the writing of the play, *Four Saints in Three Acts*.

Four Saints is a play in which language and structure oppose the dynamic thrust of performance, a play which emphasises the static qualities of language and of the written text. The text initiates a performance; it provides the songs for singing, the words for speaking. It sketches out action and the spaces in which the action can take place. At the same time, it counteracts the very performance it initiates in a kind of counter-text, a written text which asserts itself at every moment of performance, a counter-text that proceeds at a slower pace than the performed text.

To counteract the momentum of performance requires a heroic effort on the part of the dramatist. In the theatre the forward march of time is inexorable. Speech and action (and in the case of opera, music) are dynamic, and they move along a continuum. However, the performance takes place in a space and is a visual as well as a temporal phenomenon. The flow of speech and action is checked, as it were, by the way the eye perceives the performance in space – instant by instant. Really then, the dynamism of performance, while it is continuous, is more like a succession of present instants than a seamless flow. It is at once continuous and discontinuous.

The actor, the set and the text can either increase continuity or decrease it. Usually the text will provide informational connections across time. The bits of information will cohere, and their coherence will provide a kind of continuity. The use of the same set from one scene to another will also provide continuity. The actor is perhaps the source of greatest continuity in a performance. He is *in propria persona* always present and always the same. He occupies space, and he continues. He is present to the eye in each separate moment of performance, but he is also the conduit of speech and action on their journey forward through time.

In *Four Saints* Stein emphasises the discontinuity of performance rather than its continuity. Her language is static and her syntax fractured. The structure of the written text seems to militate against the actor in his role as conduit of the current of performance. Stein tries to minimize the intervention of the actor, to oppose his dynamism, and, in a sense, to prevent him from acting. What Stein tries to attain in *Four Saints* is a direct contact with her audience, without intermediary. In other words, she tries to write the actor out of *Four Saints* and to write the writer into it.

As Richard Bridgman has noted, 'almost two-thirds of the text [of *Four Saints*] is composed of authorial statement and commentary'.[8] At the beginning of the play Stein maintains a running commentary on the writing process (and progress): self-criticism, self-encouragement, progress reports, plans and preparations for writing, and discussions of the difficulty or ease of writing. She even includes dates to mark the course of her composition: April 1, Easter. The process of composition is as palpable as the procession of Saints in Act 3. Once the play gets well underway, once Saint Ignatius and Saint Therese begin to speak, Stein does not so much discuss the text that is being written or urge herself to write more of it, as deal with the written text as a plan for performance. However, it is a plan which is never settled because we are meant to see the writing and the performance as simultaneous acts.

There are a Saint Plan and a Saint Settlement among the cast of characters, and the necessity of planning and settling is brought up at intervals throughout the play, most often when Stein or her saints are having difficulty in deciding how the plan is to be settled. The refrain, 'How many saints are there in it?', is one of many similar questions: 'How many acts are there in it?' 'How many nails are there in it?' 'How many floors are there in it?' 'How many doors?' 'How many windows?' and 'How much of it is finished?' 'It is easy to measure a settlement', says Saint Therese (O&P 30). But it is not easy to measure this play because it is never settled.

The question of how many saints are in the play has several answers, all of which skirt the issue:

Saint Therese.	How many saints are there in it.
Saint Therese.	There are very many many saints in it.
Saint Therese.	There are as many saints as there are in it.
Saint Therese.	How many saints are there in it.

Saint Therese.   There are there are there are saints saints
   in it. [Stein then names seven saints, hardly a complete
   list]
Saint Therese.   How many saints are there in it.
Saint Cecilia.   How many saints are there in it.
Saint Therese.   There are as many saints as there are
   in it.
Saint Cecilia.   There are as many saints as there are
   saints in it. (O&P 28)

As for the number of acts, the title promises us three, but
the title, written first, cannot possibly measure the play,
which has not yet been written. In fact, the play has four
named acts, but there are three first acts, two second acts,
two third acts and one fourth act, making a total of eight
acts. The only certainty regarding the number of acts in
the play is that which is obvious at the end: 'Last Act. /
Which is a fact'. No matter how many acts there are in
it, the play is certain to finish. It is only when the play is
finished that we will know how many acts there were in it,
just as the number of doors, windows, floors and nails in a
house cannot be ascertained until the building is complete,
for even the most carefully laid plans can be changed.

Four Saints is certainly pre-planned. The written text
exists, and it is the plan which a performance will follow.
However, we are made to feel that the plan is being created
in our presence as the performance proceeds. Stein writes
the play so that during performance she will seem to be
feeding the actors their lines. So, for example, Stein will
write a statement, 'Who settles a private life', which is then
supposed to be echoed by an actor – 'Saint Therese. Who
settles a private life'. The imposition of the written text
on the performance text occurs also with the act/scene
divisions of *Four Saints*, most often by making the act/scene
announcement twice, once in writing and once (sometimes
more than once) in performance. For example:

Act One

Saint Therese.   Preparing in as you might say.
Saint Therese was pleasing. In as you might say.
Saint Therese Act One.
Saint Therese has begun to be in act one.
Saint Therese and begun.
Saint Therese as sung.
Saint Therese act one.
Saint Therese and begun.
Saint Therese and sing and sung.
Saint Therese in an act one. Saint Therese
    questions. (O&P 23)

and:

Scene II

Would it do if there was a Scene II. (O&P 24)

In the second example Stein discusses only the possibility
of having a Scene 2: 'Would it do?' *Four Saints* abounds in
the use of conditionals, adding to the sense of uncertainty
and tentativeness in the play. If a Scene 2 would not do,
would Stein eliminate it? As might be expected, uncertainty
is most intense in the first half of the play. As the play
takes shape it leaves fewer questions unanswered. But in
Act 1, almost nothing has been determined. Stein engages
in prolonged digressions on the disposition of the actors on
the stage, which the text never resolves, but which must,
of course, be resolved in performance. These digressions
proceed through a series of contradictory directions. At
the beginning of her deliberations about Saint Therese's
appearance on the stage, Stein repeats four times that Saint
Therese is seated, but following the fourth announcement,
she immediately contradicts herself: 'Saint Therese not
seated'. This direction is repeated, and then, as if to

reconcile the two statements, Stein adds 'Saint Therese not seated at once' (O&P 16). Presumably, Saint Therese is to begin by standing and is then to sit. The contradiction seems to be resolved. But another apparently enigmatic stage direction is introduced. Saint Therese is to be 'very nearly half inside and half outside outside the house'. Stein specifies that 'The garden' too is 'outside and inside of the wall'. While a garden can quite easily be split in two, a person cannot be so divided. So Saint Therese is neither in nor out, but somewhere in between. Poised on a threshold, she is, as Stein says, 'About to be' (O&P 16).

Because of contradictory directions and conditional suggestions, the writing of the play seems always to be in process. Composition becomes a performance event. The writing appears to be going on before the reader's and the spectator's eyes. At the same time, the unfinished quality of the written text, its very eventfulness, immobilizes the actors and the performance. Like Saint Therese, who is half in and half out, the performance itself is suspended in a kind of limbo. It consists entirely of preparation, beginning with a narrative which prepares for the play, followed by a play which prepares for a performance, and ending with the only fact, which is the last act.

In *Four Saints* Stein creates a kind of time warp by making the writing process a part of the performance. She blurs the temporal distinction between planning, writing and performance. Stein conflates the time of planning (past), the time of writing (past), the time of rehearsal (past) and the time of performance (present). She also synchronises these activities so that they occur at the same rate of speed. Because the sensual stimuli of performance (music, action and speech) move at a faster tempo than the conceptualizing activities (planning and writing), Stein immobilizes the former in order to accommodate the latter. We feel that all of these activities occur simultaneously in a very slow-moving present.

The Thomson arrangement of the text obscured its purpose and meaning by disguising the authorial voice and by ignoring the improvisational illusion which Stein created. Instead, the production of *Four Saints* emphasised the sensuality and musicality of the text. Of course, the play does have its musical side. Stein does provide a performance text and write some 'arias', but she never relinquishes her hold on the text, never withdraws, as the playwright usually does. 'When this you see', she writes, 'Remember me' (O&P 47). Even when the written text is allowed to become a song, Stein, the poet, is its singer. We must not ignore the fact that the arias in this opera are passages of unassigned text. Even 'Pigeons on the Grass' is a Stein song, although Thomson had Saint Ignatius sing it. This is how the aria appears in the original text:

Scene II

Pigeons on the grass alas.

Pigeons on the grass alas.

Short longer grass short longer longer shorter yellow grass Pigeons large pigeons on the shorter longer yellow grass alas pigeons on the grass.

If they were not pigeons what were they.

If they were not pigeons on the grass alas what were they. He had heard of a third and he asked about it it was a magpie in the sky. If a magpie in the sky on the sky can not cry if the pigeon on the grass alas can alas and to pass the pigeon on the grass alas and the magpie in the sky on the sky and to try and to try alas on the grass alas the pigeon on the grass the pigeon on the grass and alas. They might be very well very well very well they might be they might be very well they might be very well very well they might be. (O&P 36)

In an interview, Stein explained the genesis of this aria:

> I was walking in the gardens of the Luxembourg in Paris. It was the end of summer the grass was yellow. I was sorry that it was the end of summer and I saw the big fat pigeons in the yellow grass and I said to myself, pigeons on the yellow grass, alas, and I kept on writing pigeons on the grass, alas, short longer grass, short longer longer shorter yellow grass pigeons large pigeons on the shorter longer yellow grass, alas pigeons on the grass, and I kept on writing until I had emptied myself of the emotion.[9]

By incorporating the moment of creation and the improvised product of that moment into the work to be performed, Stein once again violates the temporal boundaries between the creation of the written text and its performance.[10]

The representation of the process of composing in the composition violates the most basic dramatic convention: that a play is a fictive utterance which is detached from the circumstances and conditions of its creation. In violating this convention by making *Four Saints* represent the historically unique event of its creation, Stein shows that, in fact, the only process of which a play can be the natural utterance is the process of composition, that all other mimeses are false representations. Of course, once Stein's words are committed to paper, the process becomes a product. If the product is a play, its enactment again and again, its recurrence, is guaranteed. Its detachment from the creator and the circumstances of its creation is assured. Stein's mimesis is as much an illusion as any other. To sustain this illusion Stein makes her play like a landscape, a space in which time stands still. In this landscape she preserves the historically unique moment of composition.

To the doubting, those who would insist that time cannot stand still in a play and does not in *Four Saints*, Stein offers the following parable:

> Magpies are in the landscape that is they are in the sky of a landscape, they are black and white. . . . When they are in the sky they do something that I have never seen any other bird do they hold themselves up and down and look flat against the sky.
>
> A very famous French inventor of things that have to do with stabilisation in aviation told me that what I told him magpies did could not be done by any bird but anyway whether the magpies at Avila do do it or do not at least they look as if they do do it. They look exactly like the birds in the Annunciation pictures the bird which is the Holy Ghost and rests flat against the side sky very high. (LIA 129)

Despite the doubts of the expert, the hapless French inventor who serves as her foil, Stein maintains that moving birds stand still against the sky. Impossible? Perhaps, but then Stein insists only that the birds seem stationary. Stein perceives them so because she has seen paintings in which such birds are indeed two-dimensional and inanimate and therefore can rest flat against the sky. It is not too fanciful to see Stein's feat in *Four Saints* as comparable to the immobilization of the magpie in the paintings of the Annunciation. Through her 'black and white' birds, the words of her text, she conveys an impression of stasis convincing enough to affect our perception of her play in performance. When the written words exist as perceptible and energetic language (live birds), they still appear motionless, as do the stage activities they instigate. In this illusionary landscape, where words make time stand still, we can see Gertrude Stein, the playwright, at work.

II   Schizologues: 1928–33

The new beginning in playwriting which Stein made in 1927 with *Four Saints* was not immediately productive.

She wrote only three plays in 1928 and none in 1929. In summer 1927, while working on *Four Saints*, Stein had begun the novel *Lucy Church Amiably*, the composition of which was to extend well into 1929. During 1928 and 1929 Stein was also preoccupied with the leasing and renovation of a summer house in the country at Bilignin. She and Alice finally moved into the house in spring 1929 after prolonged and complicated manœuvres to lease the property. Moreover, between 1927 and 1929 Stein composed five of the eight essays which make up *How to Write* (published in 1931), accounting for 338 of the book's 395 pages. Stein's concentration on these projects explains perhaps not only the lull in playwriting but also the overall scarcity of short works composed in any genre during these years.

Although Stein wrote few plays from 1927 to 1929, she continued in *How to Write* to explore the twin themes of language in space and language in time, the same themes that had surfaced in *A List*, in *Four Saints* and in other lang-scape plays. In *How to Write*, however, Stein was concerned not with language in the theatre but with language in books, not with performance but with writing. In *How to Write* she opposes, not the dynamism of performance, but the dynamism of language itself, its linearity and continuity. How to hold each word still, like the painted birds of the Annunciation, how to prevent the connection of one word to another and how to halt the forward-moving flight of sentences were matters Stein tried to resolve in *How to Write*.

In *How to Write* Stein discusses three components of writing: vocabulary, sentences and paragraphs. For Stein the most 'agreeable' sentences are 'successions of words' in which 'every word is at one time' (142). What Stein means by 'succession' is not continuity but contiguity. One word lies next to the other, but there are no logical or grammatical connections between words.

Through most of *How to Write* Stein questions the
necessity of grammar in the creation of sentences. 'The
question is if you have a vocabulary have you any need
of grammar except for explanation that is the question,
communication and direction repetition and intuition that
is the question' (60). Obviously, we do need grammar if we
are to communicate and to explain. The sentence is 'very
hard to save' (30) from the tyranny of grammar, precisely
because 'it is impossible to avoid meaning and if there is
meaning and it says what it does there is grammar' (71).

In Stein's opinion, however, to accept grammar is to
sacrifice that 'agreeable' succession of words in which
each component is given equal value. There are 'no words
in grammar' (54). 'Grammar is a conditional expanse'
(55) which limits language by establishing rules for the
placement of words in the expanse of the sentence. The
limitations imposed by grammar have to do with 'continuity' (61), with 'origin' (95) and with 'following after' (98),
in other words with syntagmatic relationships. Grammar
makes language a temporal medium: 'Grammar makes
dates' (57) and 'A sentence means that there is a future'
(71). Stein is inclined to think of language spatially. For
her the ideal sentence '. . . makes not it told but it hold.
A hold is where they put things' (29). 'A sentence has
nothing to do about words. . . . It has nothing to do with
them' (142). Again, 'every word is at one time' (142). The
ideal sentence is simply a 'wedding', the physical joining of
words in space.

Everything Stein has to say about sentences in *How to
Write* is extended by analogy to paragraphs. A paragraph is
composed of sentences, as a sentence is composed of words.
Like a sentence, a paragraph should obey no rules. But
what are the rules governing paragraphs? They are certainly
less rigid, less codified than the rules of grammar. They
are also therefore less abstract, less formal. A paragraph
expresses and develops an idea or an emotion, and its

form is determined only by the scope of the thought or feeling and by the intentions of the writer. In the sense that they are emotive, Stein calls paragraphs 'emotional'. But paragraphs not only register and convey emotions; they also limit them. Paragraphs set boundaries on expression. The rules of paragraphing, although not as formalized as those of grammar, dictate the length and the strategy of the paragraph – when to begin and when to end, and how to connect the sentences within it. Stein wants to do away with these rules. 'A paragraph is a liberty and a liberty is in between' (139). Not content with saving the sentence, Stein wishes to liberate the paragraph. A paragraph should be a 'succession' or a 'series of sentences' (136). The 'in between', the connection of the sentences in a paragraph and the rhetorical transitions which connect contiguous paragraphs, should be eliminated. If a paragraph were merely a space in which to arrange the 'paraphanelia' of sentences (139), it would be neither a limitation nor a development of those sentences. It would not sacrifice immediate expression to the demands of logical continuity, as does the conventional paragraph. It would neither attenuate expression nor limit its unstructured flow. As the sentence should be a 'hold' for words, the paragraph should be a 'hold' for sentences. In fact, in *How to Write* there are no conventional paragraphs. The text is divided into blocks of sentences, but as for units of expression, Stein asserts 'A sentence is our paragraph' (116).

According to Stein, sentences, unlike paragraphs, are not emotional. In her lecture 'Plays' Stein claims to have discovered in *How to Write* this fundamental difference between paragraphs and sentences:

In a book I wrote called How To Write I made a discovery which I considered fundamental, that sentences are not emotional and that paragraphs are. I found out about language that paragraphs are emotional and sentences are not and I found out something else about it. I found out that this difference was not a contradiction but a combination and that this combination causes one to think endlessly about sentences and paragraphs because the emotional paragraphs are made up of unemotional sentences. (LIA 93)

It is in combination that unemotional sentences make emotional paragraphs. The nature of individual units is altered when the units combine to form larger units: 'These are not sentences they are a part of a paragraph' (167). Stein wished to preserve the singularity of the parts, to prevent the parts from merging, connecting or combining. She did not wish to compromise the spatial integrity of each unit by sacrificing it to the temporal flow of discourse. Her prescription for 'how to write' words and sentences so that they are 'at one time' is to avoid the natural tendency to make larger units accretions of smaller units – sums of parts.

While she was working on *How to Write* and subsequently, Stein applied the instructions generated in *How to Write* to the writing of plays. In doing so, she had to come to terms with the difference between spoken and written language. As Roman Jakobson writes, 'The former has a purely temporal character, whereas the latter connects time and space. While the sounds that we hear disappear, when we read we usually have immobile letters before us and the time of the written flow of words is reversible'.[11] What Stein tries to do in her schizologues is to give the spoken language a spatial character. She had tried this once before in *A List* and its sister texts; in the schizologues she proceeds along a different track toward the same goal. As she had opposed the momentum of performance in *Four Saints*, she now opposes the momentum of language to a degree that makes the text of *Four Saints* look like a model of coherence and continuity. Through extreme discontinuity and fragmentation in all areas of the text, words and the moments of performance in which they are uttered do exist 'one at a time'. They are only here and now, connected neither to past nor to future words and moments. The result of Stein's efforts is that many of these plays are difficult to comprehend and even more difficult to enact, even with 'music to help them'.[12]

'In order for the utterance to be understood', writes Jakobson, 'attention to the flow of speech must be combined with moments of "simultaneous synthesis". . . . This is the process of unifying the elements that have already disappeared from immediate perception with those that already belong to memory. These elements are then combined into larger groupings: sounds into words, words into sentences, and sentences into utterances'.[13] Naturally, plays which frustrate this process will not play well in the theatre where they effectively turn away from the audience and its interpretive and affective response to the play.

One of the first plays written 'under the influence' of *How to Write* was *Puiseu. A Play. A Work of Pure Imagination in Which No Reminiscences Intrude* (1928). As its title suggests, it is about the *pays*: rural pursuits – sowing, reaping, winnowing; rural geography – clouds, trees, hillsides, marshes, gardens; and rural flora and fauna. But it is about these subjects in the same way that *Four Saints* is about saints. In *Paiseu* Stein is far more preoccupied with names than she is with the bucolic setting and the homely activities she includes in her play. Names appear in almost every line of text.

In her meditations on grammar in *How to Write*, Stein had not neglected names and their grammatical next of kin, nouns. She described a noun as 'the name of anything' (130). But she objected to the reversal of the axiom: 'A name and a noun is not the same that is a great discovery. A name is a place and a time a noun is once in awhile' (207); 'A name is not a noun because they will think that

Ellen means something so it does for instance' (189). A name, then, has no 'meaning' beyond the one instance of its application to a particular person or place. That makes a name an exciting and perfect word because it can never grow stale like the recurring noun. Because it comes 'once in awhile' a noun loses its correspondence to a particular place and time, loses its singularity and becomes a generalization, loses its concrete spatiality, as it were, and becomes an abstraction.

Previously, in *A List*, Stein had considered the relationship between a name in a play text and an object or person in performance. In that play Stein showed that the name is primordial, that the objects in the theatre have no existence unless their names first exist in the text. In *Paiseu* she makes a similar case for the primacy of names, but here she severs the connection between name and performance object. Here the names are objects themselves, and as such they are not generalizable from one appearance to the next and thus cannot be represented continuously or recurrently during the performance.

As I noted earlier in my discussion of *A List*, a name in a play text corresponds to an imaginary being who exists only in the playwright's mind. The only way this imaginary being can become real, can exist in performance, is through the text. He does this by speaking and by being spoken of. In *Paiseu* none of the names speaks; so named beings cannot be known in that way. But the names are spoken of. They are subjects in sentences where they are attached to predications about the person named. Thus, in *Paiseu* we hear of someone named Geronimo 'in season', 'invited', and 'in rejoinder' (LO&P 155–7). We learn, among other things, that 'Geronimo makes a middle', that he 'makes mended marshes' and that he 'has all patience here' (LO&P 158); we learn that he 'is curiously careless'; that he 'felt the need of our support' (LO&P 159) – and much, much more. (Geronimo is the most frequently occurring name in the play.) However, Stein prevents us from generalizing from these particles of information about Geronimo. Each predication is 'at one time', without continuity, without eventual summation. Therefore, although it may perform the grammatical function of a noun, the name retains its special status as a word without the accumulated, adherent meaning that normally comes from words in context.

Since the names in *Paiseu* correspond directly to the person named and have no generalized significance, they may be brought together spatially (in the 'hold' of a sentence, for instance) without merging conceptually. Let us take the ubiquitous 'Geronimo', for example. Geronimo is the given name of a 'character' in *Paiseu*. Additionally, the name Geronimo serves as a kind of surname for eighty other individuals in the play, as in Gerald Geronimo, Gabrielle Geronimo, Joseph Geronimo and Edgar Arthur Henry Edward Allen Russell Geronimo. The names 'Gerald', 'Joseph', 'Henry', 'Russell', and so forth represent separate 'characters', referred to at least once by given name only.

A shared surname usually signifies a familial, ethnic or categorical affinity among those who share it. Not so in *Paiseu*. The juxtaposition of names indicates nothing more than contiguity in a written text. The names 'Edgar Arthur Henry Edward Allen Russell Geronimo' take the singular verb 'whistles' because they share the same space in the sentence; they are parts of a collective subject, the performers of a single activity – whistling. However, the proximity of the names does not blur the distinctions between them as singular objects. If we imagine instead a sentence which reads, 'Happy, handsome, nervous, blue-eyed, pleasant Allen whistles', or 'Son, brother, husband, expatriate, lawyer, neighbour Allen whistles', we can see the difference between names and other words. Each word in our two imaginary sentences contributes to a total concept which builds gradually as the sentence proceeds; each word adds a new piece of information to the whole. This does not happen in the succession of names leading up to the verb 'whistles'. The names are together, but they do not merge. They do not 'add up'. For this reason, names are Stein's model words, exactly the kind of vocabulary she called for in *How to Write*.

As much as names in *Paiseu* frustrate synthesis and instrumentality, they are, nonetheless, parts of sentences and thus they do not escape from the inevitable linear movement in which the sentence involves them. In subsequent plays Stein was to struggle not only against synthesis but also against linearity.

First she began to place periods after the subjects of her sentences, after the names. There is one such 'sentence' in *Paiseu*: 'Rudolph Geronimo. Is never mistaken' (LO&P 158). This format was to become the mainstay of the plays of the early thirties. With a single mark of punctuation, the subject of the sentence becomes its speaker, and the sentence is rendered incomplete. When an entire play is written in this way, the normal division of a dramatic text into side text and main text forces an additional discontinuity – that between parts of a sentence. Each utterance in such a play is a fragment. The linear movement of the sentence is effectively disrupted by the conventional bifurcation of the play text.

As she uses the period to separate subject and predicate, speaker and utterance, Stein also uses it to fragment the spoken lines, as in the following from *They Must. Be Wedded. To Their Wife*:

Julia.	It is rightly. That is it. Or. That it is. Or that. Is it.
Josephine.	By which. They wish.
Julia.	And full of. Might they. Be. Without. A calling of. More than they. Further.
Josephine.	Should have thought likely.

Therese.   It is. A credit. And a pleasure.

(LO&P 229)

In this way Stein disrupts grammatical continuity and, if we imagine the appropriate breath stops at each period, slows the onrush of speech, allowing each word its full value as 'vocabulary'.

Stein often pursued such discontinuity to extreme lengths. For instance, again from *They Must. Be Wedded*:

Therese.   With their address.
Therese.   But which they will.
Therese.   But she. May be. Very well fitted.
Therese.   To be clothed. For the winter.
Therese.   To be. Admittedly. Not. In pretension.
Therese.   Nor as well. (LO&P 237)

Since all six lines are spoken by Therese, the repetition of her name is an unnecessary and annoying intrusion for the reader. It is, however, extremely effective in disrupting the linear progress of language. Our pursuit of linear succession is thwarted by the repeated shifting of our eyes back to that superfluous but insistent name.

In writing, Stein could use punctuation and the physical placement of words on the page to interfere with spatial and grammatical linearity. The visual effect of Therese's name on the reader's rate and mode of comprehension can be matched in performance by the assignment of the various fragments of a sentence or a thought to several speakers, with a comparable effect on the listener. This promised to be far more reliable as a source of discontinuity in performance than the pause suggested by a period, and far more effective. In combination, as in the following from *They Must. Be Wedded*, the two devices successfully disrupt the natural continuity of utterance:

Therese.   She will.

Julia.	Adhere. To her family.
Therese.	She will.
Josephine.	Be even pleased.
Therese.	To have them come.
Josephine.	To have been. Left. To them.
Therese.	As they will manage.
Julia.	But which they.
Josephine.	Will suggest. (LO&P 237)

Stein created entire plays out of this sort of schizologue where the human voice assists her in breaking up grammatical sentences into discontinuous segments.

Stein further thwarts the forward flow of natural utterance by making her performance text a patchwork of voices. In *They Must. Be Wedded* we find on a single page of text the following instructions for the combination, separation and recombination of voices: Josephine and Therese speak at once, then Josephine and Julia, followed by Julia and Therese, Therese again with Josephine and then again with Julia. Julia and Ernest then join voices and are eventually joined by Therese (LO&P 213–14). The fragmentation of the written text has in this way a corresponding vocal fragmentation. The names are not only seen as words on a page, but are heard as voices speaking in constantly shifting configurations. (This idea may have been suggested to Stein in part by Virgil Thomson's scoring of her texts for various voices and by his insistence in *Four Saints* on the necessity of parcelling out speeches, breaking them up for greater musical interest.)

Not only does Stein specify shifts in the combination of voices, she also indicates that there will be shifts in the speaker/listener relationship. So, for example, we have the following sequence: Josephine speaks, then Therese; Josephine then speaks to Therese; Therese and Francis speak simultaneously, then Therese alone addresses Josephine; Josephine in turn addresses Ernest and then John (LO&P 214). To be noticeable, this designation of speaker and listener must be indicated in performance by some sort of physical shift of attention. Therese must turn away from Ernest to John or perform some equivalent action in order to inform the audience that she means to address her remarks to one and not to the other. In both the shifting of vocal combinations and the shifting of attention, the written 'poetry' of character names translates into a poetry of performance. The actors in these plays serve to convey Steinian grammar and poetry and to create a performance as discontinuous as the written text from which it is extracted.

Stein also uses setting to the same effect. In a play ironically called *An Historic Drama in Memory of Winnie Elliot* Stein uses incessant scene changes to intensify the fragmentation caused by the rapid alternation of voices. This play is one of a trilogy with *Second Historic Drama. In the Country* and *Third Historic Drama*. Stein will have her fun with us, calling dramas in which temporal continuity is thwarted 'historic', invoking memory and sequence in the titles of three plays where nothing continues from one to the other except character names. A brief glance at Act 1 of the first play of the trilogy and a catalogue of the changes in scene which take place within forty-four lines of text are a sufficient demonstration of Stein's method. Scene changes occur with the following frequency: the act opens 'Inside of a room' (three lines of speech follow), then 'Leaving together' (two lines of speech), 'Out of the house' (eight lines of speech), 'In the house' (seven lines of speech), 'A street where they are building' (four lines of speech), 'A building which is not finished' (seven lines of speech), 'After they left' (four lines of speech), 'Partly at the door' (four lines of speech), 'At the door' (five lines of speech) (LO&P 182–4). This pace continues unabated through all three plays of the trilogy.

In the schizologues Stein tried, as she had in *Four Saints*, to make time stand still in the theatre. She treats the performance text like a written text, striving not for natural utterance or for word music but for a condition approaching the potential immobility of a written text where each word can exist 'at one time'. The performance is meant to exhibit the language to the audience one bit at a time. No synthesis is possible. Most of these plays would try the patience of an audience because they fight the very nature of utterance and performance and therefore frustrate the expectations and normal activities of the spectator. If these plays tell us anything about writing for the theatre, it is that in dramatic literature more than in any other literary medium, time cannot be vanquished.

Stein's names will be attached to actors, and they will speak and act as is their wont. As she writes in *A Manoir*, 'All the characters come in and are eventful' (LO&P 281). They 'come and go', 'commence to mingle and gather', do 'a great deal of work', and all of this activity 'introduces conversation' (LO&P 278–9). Like a play which is a static object, a text, 'A manoir may be built of stones and covered with mortar', may simply be an edifice (LO&P 285). But a play is also a home for actors, as a manoir is 'a house for a gentleman' (LO&P 281), 'a temporary home' (LO&P 279). Once Stein's play is inhabited (performed), it is animated. Because of the actors, performance is eventful; it involves the immobile text in history, which Stein reminds herself in *A Manoir*, 'takes time', and 'makes memory' (LO&P 279). Language in performance, even Gertrude Stein's language, is 'historic' after all.

Epilogue

In all her writing, Stein's interest was to push the limits of her medium. She made printed texts which preserved and conveyed the process of their own composition, thereby defying the conventional literary sacrifice of process to product. She used an opaque language which asserted its materiality at every turn, thereby challenging the use of language in literature as a transparent instrument of representation. She confronted each genre she used, probing its rules, problems and paradoxes. Her work embodies her critique of, her ideas about and her deconstruction of literature. A Stein text is at once a work of art and a work of criticism; in it, the writer is at once creating and thinking about creation.

Such work is difficult to read. It demands of its readers patience, open-mindedness and perseverance. Stein's work will not support a traditional exegesis because it cannot be reduced to messages or even to themes about the world outside the text. In fact, it demonstrates that knowing about the external world and telling that knowledge or reflecting that world through literature (sending messages) is often difficult and not always desirable. Stein's writing demands therefore new critical theory hospitable to the uncertainties engendered by the text. Fortunately, in post-structuralist and feminist criticism we have the tools to unlock and appreciate Stein's texts, and as a consequence, they are receiving increasingly sophisticated and clarifying critical attention.

Stein's writing rewards our reading. The verbs I have used to characterize Stein's creative activity – to question, to confront, to investigate, to explore, to push, to defy, to challenge – apply as well to the effect of her writing on the habits of readers. Because it displays the courage of its creator and the energy of its creation, Stein's writing is exhilarating. We marvel that a writer would take such risks. Nowhere are those risks more apparent than in the plays. The theatre is such a public venue. How can a text which is a personal, private, poetic investigation of language and genre work in the theatre? Yet many of these plays have been successfully performed, and even the 'failures' can pose questions we have not previously considered about theatre and about writing for the theatre. The same can be said for any of Stein's works that may appear at first reading to be 'failures' when measured by the conventional standards of their genre.

Stein's questioning and consequent dismantling not only of literary conventions but of all systems of order set her apart from other modernists in the Anglo-American tradition – Woolf, Joyce, Eliot and Pound, for example. Although the writing of these modernists represents the fragmentation, alienation, and moral relativity of their time, it also expresses their yearning for abiding and sustaining structures – myth, tradition, art. Their belief in these structures consoles them, and their works reflect and preserve the liberal humanist culture in which such structures are located. Stein, on the other hand, gloried in the chaos of the modern world. In *Picasso* she writes:

> The twentieth century is more splendid than the nineteenth century, certainly it is much more splendid. The twentieth century has much less reasonableness in its existence than the nineteenth century but reasonableness does not make for splendor. . . . The twentieth century is . . . a time when everything cracks, where everything is destroyed, everything isolates itself, it is a more splendid thing than a period where everything follows itself. (87)

Stein was no Eliot, shoring fragments against her ruins. Rather, she gleefully threw the fragments of the twentieth century into the sky above her and watched in fascination as they settled where they would on the earth below.

Stein's delight in disorder is not surprising given the influence on her of the cubist æsthetic of fragmentation. Cubist experiments with volume and form exploded the syntax of pictorial representation. A cubist painting does not reproduce familiar pictorial conventions (proportion, perspective, and chiaroscuro, for example), nor does it hold a mirror up to nature. Rather it holds a mirror to the artist's conceptualizing activities as he contemplates the external world and analyses its forms. The cubist painting reproduces that process of analysis. As David Antin has written, 'Of all the writers in English only Gertrude Stein seems to have had a thorough understanding of how profoundly Cubism opened up the possibilities of *representation*'.[1]

Seen in the context of the Anglo-American, modernist literary tradition, Stein is an outsider, an anomaly. Seen in the context of the European avant-garde of her time, however, she is nothing strange. As the only American writer to adopt the new representational strategies of cubism and to embody in her work the experimental energy of the avant-garde in pre-war Paris, Stein has had a tremendous influence on postmodern American writers, such as Richard Foreman, Robert Creeley, Robert Duncan, John Ashbery, William Gass, David Antin, John Cage, Allan Kaprow, Jerome Rothenberg and Lyn Hejinian, to name the most obvious.[2] As many of them acknowledge, she is their only literary precursor. Most of these writers are themselves radical practitioners of the language arts, members of an avant-garde that has often been marginalized by the academy and the critical establishment. Stein's lifelong willingness to leap into the unknown and to engage in experiments that might not immediately find an audience serves as a model of avant-garde activity. Stein did, however, believe that if a creator perseveres in expressing her vision, the public will catch up to her and will accept what it once rejected, recognizing it as a realization of things as they are and even seeing the beauty in that realization. Her faith in this 'reunion' of artist and audience makes her a heroic figure for the American avant-garde who not only create new literature, but new audiences as well.

Notes

Notes to Chapter 1

1. Alfred Stieglitz to Dorothy Norman, quoted in *Alfred Stieglitz: An American Seer*, by Dorothy Norman (Random House, 1960), pp. 110–11.

2. Ibid., pp. 111–12.

3. Stein mentions the Stieglitz visit and their subsequent discussion of the visit in *Everybody's Autobiography*, p. 72.

4. Alice Toklas, *What Is Remembered* (Holt, Rinehart and Winston, 1963), p. 23.

5. Agnes Ernst Meyer, *Out of These Roots* (Little Brown, 1953), p. 81. Quoted in James Mellow, *Charmed Circle: Gertrude Stein & Company* (Praeger, 1974), p. 16.

6. Hutchins Hapgood, *A Victorian in the Modern World* (Harcourt Brace, 1939), p. 131. Quoted in Mellow, *Charmed Circle*, p. 209.

7. Leo Stein, *Journey into the Self, Being the Letters, Papers and Journals of Leo Stein*, ed. Edmund Fuller (Crown Publishers, 1950), pp. 185 7.

8. Shari Benstock, *Women of the Left Bank, Paris, 1900–1940* (University of Texas Press, 1986), pp. 145–6.

9. In the Virago Edition of *Everybody's Autobiography* 'initiative' has been misprinted 'initiation'.

10. Although it is called *The Autobiography of Alice B. Toklas* and told as a first–person autobiographical narrative, Gertrude Stein was in fact the author of this 'autobiography' of another woman, her lifelong mate, Alice Toklas.

11. Leo Stein to Gertrude Stein, 20 December 1900, *Journey into the Self*, p. 5.

12. Ibid., p. 5.

13. Quoted in a letter from Mrs. Michael Stein to Gertrude Stein, 20 January 1897, *The Flowers of Friendship: Letters Written to Gertrude Stein*, ed. Donald Gallup (Alfred A. Knopf, 1953), p. 12.

14. Maurice Sterne, *Shadow and Light* (Harcourt Brace, 1965), p. 53. Quoted in Mellow, *Charmed Circle*, p. 17.

15. Leo Stein to Mabel Weeks, 19 September 1902, *Journey Into the Self*, p.13.

16. Mellow, *Charmed Circle*, p. 27.

17. Rosalind Miller, *Gertrude Stein: Form and Intelligibility* (Exposition Press, 1949), p. 146. Miller reprints all of the essays and stories Stein wrote for her English classes at Harvard.

18. See Richard Bridgman, *Gertrude Stein in Pieces* (Oxford University Press, 1970), pp. 133–4; S. C. Neuman, *Gertrude Stein: Autobiography and the Problem of Narration* (University of Victoria, 1979), chapter 3; Lisa Ruddick, *Reading Gertrude Stein: Body, Text, Gnosis* (Cornell University Press, 1990), chapter 1; Wendy Steiner, *Exact Resemblance to Exact Resemblance: The Literary Portraiture of Gertrude Stein* (Yale University Press, 1978), chapter 2; Donald Sutherland, *Gertrude Stein: A Biography of Her Work* (Yale University Press, 1951), pp. 1–13; and Jayne L. Walker, *The Making of a Modernist: Gertrude Stein from Three Lives to Tender Buttons* (The University of Massachusetts Press, 1984), chapters 1 and 5.

19. Leo Stein, *Journey Into the Self*, p. 194.

20. Bridgman, *Gertrude Stein in Pieces*, p. 35; Mellow, *Charmed Circle*, p. 44; and Benstock, *Women of the Left Bank*, p. 147.

21. Leo Stein to Albert Barnes, 20 October 1934, *Journey Into the Self*, p. 148.

22. Dr. Lewellys Barker to Gertrude Stein, 30 January 1902, *Flowers of Friendship*, ed. Gallup, p. 24.

23. Leo Stein to Gertrude Stein, 3 February 1901, *Journey Into the Self*, p. 7.

24. Benstock, *Women of the Left Bank*, p. 147 and *Mellow, Charmed Circle*, p. 45.

25. Mellow, *Charmed Circle*, p. 59.

26. Bridgman, *Gertrude Stein in Pieces*, p. 45.

27. Although Stein was Jewish, she identified herself as an American and a westerner, but not as a Jew. In all her observations about her nationality and about the elements of her character that might have their source in ethnicity, Stein almost never alludes to her Jewishness.

28. Mellow, *Charmed Circle*, p. 47.

29. Leon Katz, Introduction to *Fernhurst, Q.E.D., and Other Early Writing*, by Gertrude Stein (Liveright, 1971), p. xviii.

30. Ibid., p. xvii.

31. Sterne, *Shadow and Light*, pp. 47–9. Quoted in Mellow, *Charmed Circle*, pp. 16–17.

32. Mellow, *Charmed Circle*, p. 58 and Bridgman, *Gertrude Stein in Pieces*, p. 45.

33. In *Q.E.D.*, the Stein figure, Adele, who is travelling with her brother in Spain and Morocco, thinks about the glimpse of sexual passion she has had with Helen: 'She thought of it

as she and her brother lay in the evenings on the hill-side at Tangiers. . . . As they lay there agreeing and disagreeing in endless discussion with an intensity of interest that long familiarity had in no way diminished . . . she enjoyed to the full the sense of family friendship. She felt that her glimpse [of sexual passion] had nothing to do with all this. It belonged to another less pleasant and more incomplete emotional world' (FQED 67). It is likely that, like Adele, Gertrude Stein tried to keep that other world of her sexuality apart from the world of 'family friendship'.

34. Although Stein remembers *Young Girl with Basket of Flowers* as Leo's first purchase of a Picasso painting, he had actually a few days earlier bought *Harlequin's Family with an Ape*.

35. Picasso had no less an affinity for Stein than she for him. He was, of course, grateful for her patronage and support. But more than that, he genuinely admired poets and poetry. Stein was one of a number of poets who were his close friends and who influenced his work – Guillaume Apollinaire, Max Jacob and Jean Cocteau, for example. Moreover, according to his most recent biographer, Picasso was fascinated by large women and had a 'penchant for lesbianism' (John Richardson, *A Life of Picasso, Volume I, 1881–1906* [Random House, 1991], p. 304). For many reasons, then, Picasso was predisposed to take an interest in Stein.

36. Stein calls 'Melanctha' the second story of *Three Lives*. It is indeed the middle story in the published book, but it was the last of the three stories to be written.

37. See Roland Penrose, *Picasso: His Life and Work* (Schocken Books, 1962), pp. 114–20 and John Richardson, *A Life of Picasso*, chapter 26. Richardson gives slightly more importance to the painting of Stein's portrait than Penrose does, but both writers agree that the tendencies visible in the portrait of Gertrude Stein (the depiction of monumental women and the use of a masklike face) had other sources and did not originate during the winter in which Picasso focused so intensely on this model and this work.

38. Even when Picasso painted *Les Demoiselles d'Avignon*, a painting which at first displeased his friends and admirers, he still had the enthusiastic support of Wilhelm Uhde, the German critic and collector, and Uhde's friend, Daniel-Henry Kahnweiler, who was to replace Ambroise Vollard as Picasso's dealer. (See Penrose, *Picasso*, p. 127.)

39. Gertrude Sein to Mabel Weeks, ND. Quoted in Mellow, *Charmed Circle*, p. 77.

40. Leo Stein to Mabel Weeks, 7 February 1913, *Journey Into the Self*, pp. 52–3.

41. Benstock, *Women of the Left Bank*, p. 153.

42. Toklas, *What Is Remembered*, p. 3.

43. Ibid., pp. 41–2.

44. Ibid., p. 44.

45. Leo Stein to Mabel Weeks, 7 February 1913, *Journey Into the Self*, p. 52.

46. For feminist responses to the Stein/Toklas marriage see Benstock, *Women of the Left Bank*, pp. 18–19; Blanche Cook, 'Women Alone Stir My Imagination: Lesbianism and the Cultural Tradition', *Signs* 4 (1979) 718–39; and Carolyn G. Heilbrun, *Writing a Woman's Life* (Ballantine Books, 1988), pp. 79–80.

47. Catharine R. Stimpson, 'Gertrice/Altrude: Stein, Toklas, and the Paradox of the Happy Marriage,' in *Mothering the Mind: Twelve Studies of Writers and Their Silent Partners*, ed. Ruth Perry and Martine Watson Brownley (Holmes & Meier, 1984), pp.130–1.

Notes to Chapter 2

1. Stein once advised a young writer to 'think of the writing in terms of discovery, which is to say that creation must take place between the pen and the paper, not before in a thought or afterwards in a recasting' (John Hyde Preston, 'A Conversation', *The Atlantic Monthly* [August 1935] 187).

2. For a brilliant discussion of Stein's indeterminate (enigmatic) poetry in the context of similar twentieth-century poetry, see Marjorie Perloff, *The Poetics of Indeterminacy: Rimbaud to Cage* (Princeton University Press, 1981).

3. We know of these intentions because of the notebooks in which she planned these works (especially *The Making of Americans*). Stein's notebooks are available to scholars in the Yale Collection of American Literature, Beinecke Rare Book and Manuscript Library, Yale University, hereafter referred to as 'Yale Collection'.

4. In the published version of *Three Lives*, 'Melanctha' is the middle story, but we will consider the stories here in the order of their composition, with 'The Good Anna' the first written and 'Melanctha' the last.

5. Given the date of its composition (1905) and the prevailing taboo against the outright depiction of sexual acts, the sexual content of 'Melanctha' is, understandably, suggested indirectly through the use of euphemism and symbolism. Thus, Stein refers to Melanctha's awakening sexuality as 'her power' as a woman 'stirring within her' (86), to her sexual desire as wanting 'it' badly (87), to her promiscuity as 'wandering after wisdom' (88) and to sexual intercourse as a kind

of 'knowledge'. Stein uses trains (and men working on trains and inviting Melanctha to sit on their engines), ships (with their 'dark and smelly places') and construction sites (with their cranes and the workers' invitations to Melanctha to 'stand up here on top where I be') to symbolize male sexuality and Melanctha's flirtations as she wanders after wisdom (89–93). When Melanctha falls from a high place and breaks her arm, a metaphoric sexual initiation is hinted at. In the case of Jane Harden, it is not clear because of the indirection in the text whether Melanctha becomes her lover or just her friend, although the former is suggested by passages like the following: 'She [Jane Harden] loved Melanctha hard and made Melanctha feel *it* very deeply. She would *be with* other people and *with* men and *with* Melanctha, and *she would make Melanctha understand what everybody wanted*, and *what one did with power when one had it*' (96) (emphasis added).

6. Mary Field Belenky *et al.*, *Women's Ways of Knowing: The Development of Self, Voice, and Mind* (Basic Books, 1986), p. 144.

7. Belenky argues that 'really talking' is more characteristic of female conversation and 'didactic talking' of male, but Carol Gilligan cautions that such an 'association [between perceptual and communicative mode and gender] is not absolute' and that 'contrasts between male and female voices . . . highlight a distinction between two modes of thought . . . rather than . . . represent a generalization about either sex' (Carol Gilligan, *In a Different Voice: Psychological Theory and Women's Development* [Harvard University Press, 1982], p. 2). A similar caution is in order here. For Stein, neither style of talk represented in *Three Lives* is gender-related. Admittedly, Melanctha is, most of the time, a real talker, but Anna, Mrs. Kreder and Mrs. Haydon, all women, are all didactic talkers. Even Melanctha is sometimes a didactic talker. Both Lena and Herman are quiet listeners, despite their gender difference. Jeff, who is clearly a didactic talker, learns to become better at really talking. Moreover, Jeff is the reincarnation of *Q.E.D.*'s Adele, a woman and a didactic talker, who is in turn a surrogate for Stein, a didactic talker in some circumstances, a real talker in others and a quiet listener in still others.

8. There are clear parallels between the two styles of talk (didactic talking and really talking) and the two styles of writing which Stein described as 'writing what you intended to write' and 'writing what you are writing'. The latter type of writing requires a 'listening' to one's inner voice and an openness to exploration and discovery. Though some have argued that the new style of writing Stein was discovering was a female or feminist syle (see Harriet Scott Chessman, *The Public Is Invited to Dance: Representation, the Body, and Dialogue in Gertrude Stein* [Stanford University Press, 1989], Marianne DeKoven, *A Different Language: Gertrude Stein's Experimental Writing* [University of Wisconsin Press, 1983], and

Lisa Ruddick, *Reading Gertrude Stein*), I do not believe that the two styles of writing are necessarily gender-related, any more than the two styles of talking, and I would urge the same caution against genderizing Stein's writing style that I urged against genderizing the conversational styles of her characters.

9. Stein's technique in 'Melanctha' is not to be confused with stream of consciousness, the technique of modernists like Virginia Woolf, James Joyce and Dorothy Richardson. Stein is not following the vagaries of a character's internal thought process; rather, she records the stream of speech or language by which her characters try to make meaning and to communicate it to each other.

10. In *Re-Forming the Narrative: Toward a Mechanics of Modernist Fiction* (Cornell University Press, 1987), David Hayman points to Flaubert, and specifically to his portrait of Félicité in 'Un coeur simple', as an important precursor of the kind of novel he calls self-generating: that is, novels which 'enact, or . . . embody, their production'. He writes, 'Such texts generally present themselves as the products of an associative process that is transparently available in the very texture of the narrative . . . . The internal processes of production constitute in large measure the action of the text' (12–13). 'Melanctha' and, to a lesser extent, 'The Good Anna' and 'The Gentle Lena' are self-generating texts as my discussion of them shows. While Flaubert's 'Un coeur simple' may have suggested such a narrative strategy to Stein, she pursued this strategy to an extreme that could hardly be imagined by anyone reading Flaubert's story. Her extreme departure from the Flaubertian model was inspired by her exposure to and sympathy with the work of Cézanne and Picasso.

11. For an excellent discussion of the influence of Cézanne and Picasso on Stein see Jayne Walker, *The Making of a Modernist*. See also Charles Altieri, *Painterly Abstraction in Modernist American Poetry: The Contemporaneity of Modernism* (Cambridge University Press, 1989), chapters 6 and 7; Stephen Scobie, 'The Allure of Multiplicity: Metaphor and Metonymy in Cubism and Gertrude Stein', in *Gertrude Stein and the Making of Literature*, ed. Shirley Neuman and Ira B. Nadel (Northeastern University Press, 1988), pp. 98–111; and Wendy Steiner, *Exact Resemblance to Exact Resemblance*.

12. It is likely that the portrait of Mme. Cézanne was painted, as was the Stein portrait, over a long period of time and that the head was completed after a hiatus, as was the Stein head. According to John Rewald, the design of the wallpaper in the Cézanne portrait 'can be identified with lodgings Cézanne occupied in 1879–80, but the . . . head of the sitter appears to have been painted several years later' (*Cézanne, the Steins and Their Circle* [Thames and Hudson, 1986], p. 38). Of course, neither Picasso nor Stein would necessarily have known this history of the Cézanne portrait. However, they would

certainly have heard the story of Cézanne's portrait of Ambroise Vollard for which Vollard sat 115 times; after this ordeal, Cézanne 'abruptly abandoned the project, saying "the front of the shirt is not bad"' (Ian Dunlop, Introduction to *The Complete Paintings of Cézanne* [Penguin, 1985], p. 5).

Notes to Chapter 3

1. Leon Katz, 'The First Making of *The Making of Americans*', Ph.D. diss. Columbia University, 1963.

2. Leon Katz, Introduction to *Fernhurst, Q.E.D.*, by Gertrude Stein, p. xxiii.

3. The choice of the name Gossols was no doubt inspired by the name of the Spanish village, Gosol, where Picasso and his mistress Fernande spent nine weeks during the summer of 1906.

Notes to Chapter 4

1. There is some disagreement as to the dates and the order of composition of *Tender Buttons*. The Yale Catalogue dates the composition 1910–1912, but as Richard Bridgman points out, Stein herself places the composition somewhat later, thereby casting some doubt on the Yale dating (*Gertrude Stein in Pieces*, 125n). The consensus among critics is that *Tender Buttons* was written during 1911 and 1912. Although Marianne DeKoven and Lisa Ruddick argue that 'Rooms' was written in 1911 before 'Objects' and 'Food', most critics accept the order of publication as the order of composition. 'Rooms' is such an amalgam of styles that I am not convinced by the argument for its early composition. I believe that 'Rooms' was composed after 'Objects' and 'Food' and much later than is normally supposed. There is internal evidence suggesting that 'Rooms' may have been composed as late as 1914, right before Stein sent the entire manuscript to the publisher, Donald Evans, in late spring. Early in 1914, soon after Leo's permanent departure from the household, Gertrude and Alice were given permission to renovate the apartment at rue de Fleurus and so decided to remain

in residence there. They began renovations early in 1914 (possibly in February). According to Mellow, the apartment was 'wired for electricity' and a 'sheltering passageway constructed between the pavilion and the studio room . . . [which] necessitated the cutting of a new doorway' (*Charmed Circle*, p. 206). References in *Tender Buttons* to construction, to a 'passage' which is a 'pleasure . . . when every room is open' (500), to 'currents', 'on the floor' and 'in the door' and to 'a change . . . in current' (505) suggest that 'Rooms' was being written while the rooms at rue de Fleurus were being renovated. (NOTE: *Tender Buttons* was published in 1914 in New York by Claire Marie Press; it is reprinted in *Selected Writings of Gertrude Stein* [Random House, 1962], 459–509. All references to *Tender Buttons* are to *Selected Writings*).

2. In an inteview with Robert Bartlett Haas, Stein explained her 'composition' of these word paintings: 'I used to take objects on a table, like a tumbler or any kind of object and try to get the picture of it clear and separate in my mind and create a word relationship between the word and the things seen' ('A Transatlantic Interview', in *A Primer for the Gradual Understanding of Gertrude Stein*, ed. Robert Bartlett Haas [Black Sparrow Press, 1971], p. 25). While the objects on the table may have been a catalyst for the writing, I show in this chapter that the writing itself came to have more importance than the representation of the visible world.

3. Allegra Stewart, *Gertrude Stein and the Present* (Harvard University Press, 1967); Pamela Hadas, 'Spreading the Difference: One Way to Read Gertrude Stein's *Tender Buttons*', *Twentieth Century Literature* 24, I (Spring 1978) 57–75; Doris Wright, 'Woman as Eros-Rose in Gertrude Stein's *Tender Buttons* and Contemporaneous Portraits', *Transactions of the Wisconsin Academy of Sciences, Arts, and Letters* 74 (1986) 34–40; Catharine R. Stimpson, 'The Somagrams of Gertrude Stein', in *Critical Essays on Gertrude Stein*, ed. Michael J. Hoffman (G.K. Hall, 1986), pp. 183–196; Shari Benstock, *Women of the Left Bank*, pp. 161–2; Neil Schmitz, *Of Huck and Alice: Humorous Writing in American Literature* (University of Minnesota Press, 1983), pp. 162–199; William Gass, 'Gertrude Stein: Her Escape from Protective Language', in *Fictions and the Figures of Life* (Alfred A. Knopf, 1971), pp. 79–96.

4. Chessman, *The Public Is Invited to Dance*, p. 90.

5. Ruddick, *Reading Gertrude Stein*, p. 191.

6. Ibid., p. 203.

7. Ibid., p. 190.

8. Perloff, *Poetics of Indeterminacy*, p. 107.

9. Ibid., p. 85.

10. Neil Schmitz, 'Gertrude Stein as Post-Modernist: The Rhetoric of *Tender Buttons*', in *Critical Essays on Gertrude Stein*, ed. Michael J. Hoffman, p. 119.

11. Schmitz, *Of Huck and Alice*, p. 186.

12. Walker, *The Making of a Modernist*, p. 149.

13. DeKoven, *A Different Language*, p. 76.

14. Barbara Hernnstein Smith, 'Contingencies of Value', in *Canons*, ed. Robert von Hallberg (University of Chicago Press, 1983), p. 17. Smith's comments about classification, function and value appear in an essay concerned with canonical and non-canonical texts and with the system of literary evaluation by which the canon is established and questioned. Her central point is that literary value is mutable, diverse (14) and 'radically contingent' (18). I believe that *Tender Buttons* makes a similar 'point' and that it 'argues' implicitly for a system of classification in which a text like *Tender Buttons* would have value in spite of the fact that it does not serve the same function as an ode by John Keats, for example.

15. Walker, *The Making of a Modernist*, p. 132.

16. This is the reading offered by Lisa Ruddick in 'A Rosy Charm: Gertrude Stein and the Repressed Feminine', in *Critical Essays on Gertrude Stein*, ed. Michael J. Hoffman, p. 228.

17. In manuscript 'excellent' is written 'xcellent', and looking at that shorthand spelling suggests to Stein that 'easy' can also be expressed in shorthand as 'e c' (Yale Collection).

18. Ruddick, *Reading Gertrude Stein*, p. 215.

Notes to Chapter 5

1. The material in chapters 5 and 6 is adapted from my book, *'They Watch Me As They Watch This': Gertrude Stein's Metadrama* (University of Pennsylvania Press, 1991).

2. Gertrude Stein to Mabel Dodge, [?] 1913 (Yale Collection).

3. Donald Evans to Gertrude Stein, 18 February 1914, *The Flowers of Friendship*, ed. Gallup, pp. 95–6.

4. Henry McBride to Gertrude Stein, 28 August 1913, *The Flowers of Friendship*, ed. Gallup, p. 83.

5. Alice Toklas to Carl Van Vechten, 19 November 1946, *Staying on Alone: Letters of Alice B. Toklas*, ed. Edward Burns (Vintage Books, 1975), p. 32.

6. Julian Beck, 'Storming the Barricades', Introduction to *The Brig*, by Kenneth H. Brown (Hill and Wang, 1965), p. 8.

7. Quoted by Kate Davy in 'Richard Foreman's Ontological-Hysteric Theatre: The Influence of Gertrude Stein', *Twentieth*

Century Literature (Spring 1978) 108–9.

8. Keir Elam, *The Semiotics of Theatre and Drama* (Methuen, 1980), p. 138.

9. Jindřich Honzl, 'The Hierarchy of Dramatic Devices', in *The Semiotics of Art: The Prague School Contributions*, ed. Ladislav Matejka and Irwin R. Titunik (MIT Press, 1976), p.127.

10. I am using the terms 'natural' and 'fictive utterance' in the sense suggested by Barbara Herrnstein Smith in *On the Margins of Discourse* (University of Chicago Press, 1978). According to Smith, a natural utterance is 'a historical event . . . it occupies a specific and unique point in time [and] space and thus cannot recur, for it is historically unique'. A printed text that is a record of vocal utterance is not a natural utterance, but the transcription of one. Poems and plays are fictive utterances, representations of natural utterance. A written text can only be a natural utterance at the moment of its composition (pp. 15–28).

11. Gertrude Stein, *Bee Time Vine and Other Pieces* (Yale University Press, 1953), pp. 204–5.

12. Stein wrote most of the conversation plays while she and Alice Toklas lived in Mallorca where they had sought refuge from the war. As she wrote in a 1915 letter to Henry McBride, she was 'inspired by the Mallorcans a very foolish lot of decayed pirates with an awful language' (18 September 1915, Yale Collection). Undoubtedly, Stein's reproduction in her conversation plays of the give and take of social conversation was 'inspired' in part by the conversations taking place around her and by the necessary concentration on domestic life occasioned by her temporary exile from Paris. References to Mallorca, Mallorcans, islands, water, and war and its privations dot the conversation plays. While such biographical information can only enrich our reading of the plays, it should not distract us from the fact that these plays are more concerned with the form of conversation than with its meaning and that, for Stein at this time, a word's possible reference to an extralinguisitic situation was its least important feature.

13. Elam, *The Semiotics of Theatre and Drama*, p. 151.

14. Ibid., p. 182.

15. Bridgman, *Gertrude Stein in Pieces*, p. 58.

16. Susanne Langer, *Feeling and Form: A Theory of Art* (Charles Scribner's Sons, 1953), p. 310.

17. According to Betsy Alayne Ryan's 'Chronological List of Productions' (*Gertrude Stein's Theatre of the Absolute* [UMI Research Press, 1984], Appendix C, pp. 165–89), only one of the conversation plays, *For the Country Entirely*, has been produced in its entirety without operatic adaptation.

Notes to Chapter 6

1. Yi-Fu Tuan, 'Thought and Landscape: The Eye and the Mind's Eye', in *The Interpretation of Ordinary Landscapes*, ed. D. W. Meinig (Oxford University Press, 1979), p. 90.

2. John A. Jakle, *The Visual Elements of Landscape* (University of Massachusetts Press, 1987), p. 8.

3. Lawrence Kornfeld, 'From a Director's Notebook: How the Curtain Did Come: Conflict and Change: The Theatre of Gertrude Stein', *Performing Arts Journal* (Spring 1976), pp. 33–5.

4. In manuscript Stein writes 'Susan Mabel Martha and Susan, Mable and Martha and a father', changing the spelling of the second 'Mabel', an 'error' Toklas corrected when she typed the manuscript. The 'misspelling' shows that orthography also plays a part in our recognition of people by their names (Stein, *A List*, MS. 286, Yale Collection).

5. In 1923, the year that Stein wrote *A List*, Georges Pitöeff staged Luigi Pirandello's *Six Characters in Search of an Author* for Parisian audiences. In Stein's play, as in Pirandello's, the existence, identity and fate of the characters depend on the playwriting activities of the author, and this connection between authorial process and dramatic realization is debated by characters in both plays. There is no evidence that Stein saw Pirandello's play, but if she did not see it, she would have inevitably heard about it since it was a much discussed *succès de scandale*. The metatextual affinities between *A List* and *Six Characters in Search of an Author* are undeniable. The interesting difference between the two plays is that the fate of Pirandello's characters depends on the form in which the playwright will cast their story whereas the fate of Stein's characters is determined by language itself, by the way words appear in the playwright's text.

6. Despite her familiarity with opera and her awareness of parallels between certain operas and her own plays, despite her designation of three of the texts in *Operas and Plays* as operas (*Four Saints in Three Acts, A Lyrical Opera Made by Two to Be Sung* and *Madame Recamier. An Opera*) and despite Thomson's commission of an opera libretto, I will be discussing *Four Saints* not as an opera but as a play. In the first place, I see no textual characteristics to distinguish *Four Saints*, or either of the other two so-called operas, from the plays of this period. Moreover, Stein herself seems to have had trouble maintaining the generic distinction. For example, the manuscript of *Madame Recamier* bears the subtitle, 'An Opera' (*Mme Recamier An Opera* (MS. 416, Yale Collection), but when Stein mentions *Madame Recamier* in a 1930 letter to Henry McBride, she writes, 'I have written a real play a poetic meditative conversational drama about Mme Recamier, I think even the small or big theatres might act it it is so like a real play . . . a

really truly play' (25 October 1930, Yale Collection). In 'Plays' she quotes from *Madame Recamier* as one example of a 'great number of plays' (LIA 125), and later in *Everybody's Autobiography* she again calls it a play (114). Similarly, she calls *Four Saints* an 'opera' (EA 48, 98, 111, 193), a 'play' (EA 194, LIA 125, 129, 131) and a 'drama' (EA 283). *Four Saints* is not 'operatic' by virtue of any intrinsic qualities but because Thomson set the play *Four Saints* to music.

7. Stein uses the French spelling of Teresa without accent marks – Therese – throughout the play.

8. Bridgman, *Gertrude Stein in Pieces*, p. 187.

9. Gertrude Stein, typescript of a tape-recorded interview with William Lundell for the National Broadcasting Company, New York, 12 October 1934 (Yale Collection). Stein's memory is confused here. She finished the manuscript at the end of July, which is not exactly the end of summer, although the grass in this urban park could certainly have been yellow in July.

10. In addition to being Stein's lament about the yellowing grass and the end of summer, 'alas' is also a pun on Alice. Ulla Dydo, Harriet Chessman and Neil Schmitz have all discussed the omnipresence of Alice Toklas in Stein's writing. As Schmitz writes, 'She is addressed, cited, quoted . . . [she is] everywhere in Gertrude Stein's text, variously figured, differently inscribed' (*Of Huck and Alice*, p. 202). By singing in *Four Saints* to Alice/alas (the witness to the writing and the companion of the writer), Stein further draws creation and performance together.

11. Roman Jakobson, *Verbal Art, Verbal Sign, Verbal Time*, ed. Krystyna Pomorska and Stephen Rudy (University of Minnesota Press, 1985), p. 20.

12. In *Everybody's Autobiography*, writing about the Virgil Thomson/ Maurice Grosser production of *Four Saints* and about the Gerald Berners staging of *Wedding Bouquet*, Stein comments, 'As yet they have not yet done any of mine without music to help them. They could though and it would be interesting but no one has yet' (194).

13. Jakobson, *Verbal Art*, p. 20.

Notes to Epilogue

1. David Antin, 'Some Questions about Modernism', *Occident* (Spring 1874), p. 13.

2. For an excellent discussion of Stein's influence on artists, dancers and composers, and on the New York avant-garde art scene in general, see Henry M. Sayre, 'The Artist's Model: American Art and the Question of Looking like Gertrude Stein', in *Gertrude Stein and the Making of Literature*, ed. Neuman and Nadel, pp. 21–41.

Bibliography

Abbreviations are used for parenthetical references when the source of the quotation is not specified in the text. Page references in the text are to the following editions:

ABT *The Autobiography of Alice B. Toklas* (Vintage Books, 1990).

  Can You See the Name, in *Bee Time Vine and Other Pieces* (Yale University Press, 1953), pp. 204–5.

EA *Everybody's Autobiography* (Virago, 1985).

FIA *Four in America* (Books for Libraries Press, 1969).

FQED *Fernhurst, Q.E.D., and Other Early Writings* (Liveright, 1971).

  How to Write (Something Else Press, 1973).

LIA *Lectures in America* (Beacon Press, 1985).

LO&P *Last Operas and Plays* (Vintage Books, 1975).

MOA *The Making of Americans* (Something Else Press, 1972).

O&P *Operas and Plays* (Station Hill Press, 1987).

P *Picasso: The Complete Writings* (Beacon Press, 1985).

  Tender Buttons, in *Selected Writings of Gertrude Stein* (Vintage Books, 1990), pp. 459–509.

TL *Three Lives* (Penguin, 1987).

WAM *What Are Masterpieces* (Pitman Publishing, 1940).

Index